COMPLETE HOME ENTERTAINMENT FOR THE FAMILY

Music arranged and edited by
Dan Fox
Project Editor:
Joseph Abend

THIS BOOK PRODUCED FOR T. B. HARMS COMPANY
BY FUN-WITH-MUSIC CO., INC.
NEPTUNE, N. J.

LIBRARY OF CONGRESS CATALOG CARD NO. 74-17539

Exclusive Music Trade Distributor
Cimino Publications Incorporated
Farmingdale, L. I., N.Y.
H-13-890

Exclusive Book Trade Distributor
Crown Publishers, Inc.
419 Park Avenue South
New York, N.Y. 10016
0-517-521725

Alphabetical Index to Songs

Index by Category

FROM THE ALL TIME HIT PARADE

SHOW TIME HITS

GAY 90'S AND GASLIGHT FAVORITES

INTERNATIONAL FAVORITES

FILM SONGS

COUNTRY AND WESTERN

FOLK SONGS AND AMERICANA

RELIGIOUS AND PATRIOTIC SONGS

FOR THE YOUNGSTERS

LAWRENCE WELK THEME SONG

Dear Musical Friends:

I sincerely hope my new song book will help you get as much fun from *your* music making as I get from mine.

For many years I have wanted to put together a book such as this, featuring favorite songs from all fields of popular music—a book every member of the family would find enjoyable.

Well, here it is—a "do-it-yourself" fun-book for your family's playing, singing, and reminiscing pleasure.

While thinking about this book, it occurred to me that much of the popular music printed today is too difficult to play without a great deal of practice and experience; and, sometimes, written in keys uncomfortable to sing. I decided to look for an arranger who could take great songs, give them fresh, new professional-sounding arrangements and yet make them easy enough to play and sing for the average amateur music maker.

Fortunately, I found Dan Fox, a man who has had much experience in arranging for print. Dan's work is stylish and a great joy to play.

Each of Dan's arrangements is suitable for piano, organ (the small bass notes are organ pedal notes), violin, flute, oboe and guitar. The finger chart diagrams are for guitarists who may not read notes or chord symbols and, of course, the chord symbols are appropriate for other fretted instruments such as the ukulele, banjo and mandolin.

Pianists and organists who play the "popular" or chord method will also be able to play from the chord symbols. You may even be able to apply these chord symbols to certain chord organs.

If you play a bass instrument, either string or brass, you can play along by reading the root note of each chord symbol—for example: G7 Chord—play G, etc....

Accordion players can easily adapt these arrangements by playing the right hand piano part on the keyboard and the single bass notes or chords—as indicated by the chord symbols—on the buttons.

Enough technical talk—it's time for you to turn the page and have some fun by making music.

Gather everyone together—sound your "A", and have yourself a ball. Let's all become one big happy "Musical Family."

A-One . . . A-Two . . .

Lawrence Welk

FROM THE ALL TIME HIT PARADE

GOIN' OUT OF MY HEAD

Cm7
3fr
Cmaj7
5fr
Cm7
3fr
Cmaj7
5fr
C7-5
think I'm go-ing out of my head 'Cause I can't ex-plain the tears that I shed o - ver
Fmaj7
F6
Fm7
B♭9
you, o - ver you. I
E♭
3fr
Gm
3fr
E♭
3fr
Gm
3fr
A♭
B♭9
see you each morn-ing but you just walk past me you don't e - ven know that I ex -
Cmaj7
5fr
(No chords)
Cmaj7
F
ist. Go-in' out of my head o - ver you, Out of my

Cmaj7
F
Cmaj7
F
Cmaj7
F
Cmaj7
F
head o - ver you,_ Out of my head day_ and night night and day and
Cmaj7
F
Cmaj7
C
D/F♯ bass
2fr
Fm6
4fr
night wrong_ or right, I must think of a way in - to your
gradually getting softer
C/Ebass
E♭dim
G7
F♯dim/Gbass
T
heart. There's no rea - son why my be - ing shy should keep us a -
F/Gbass
G7
Cm7
3fr
Cmaj7
5fr
Repeat and fade
part. And I think I'm go-ing out of my head Yes, I

HONEY

Words and Music by
BOBBY RUSSELL

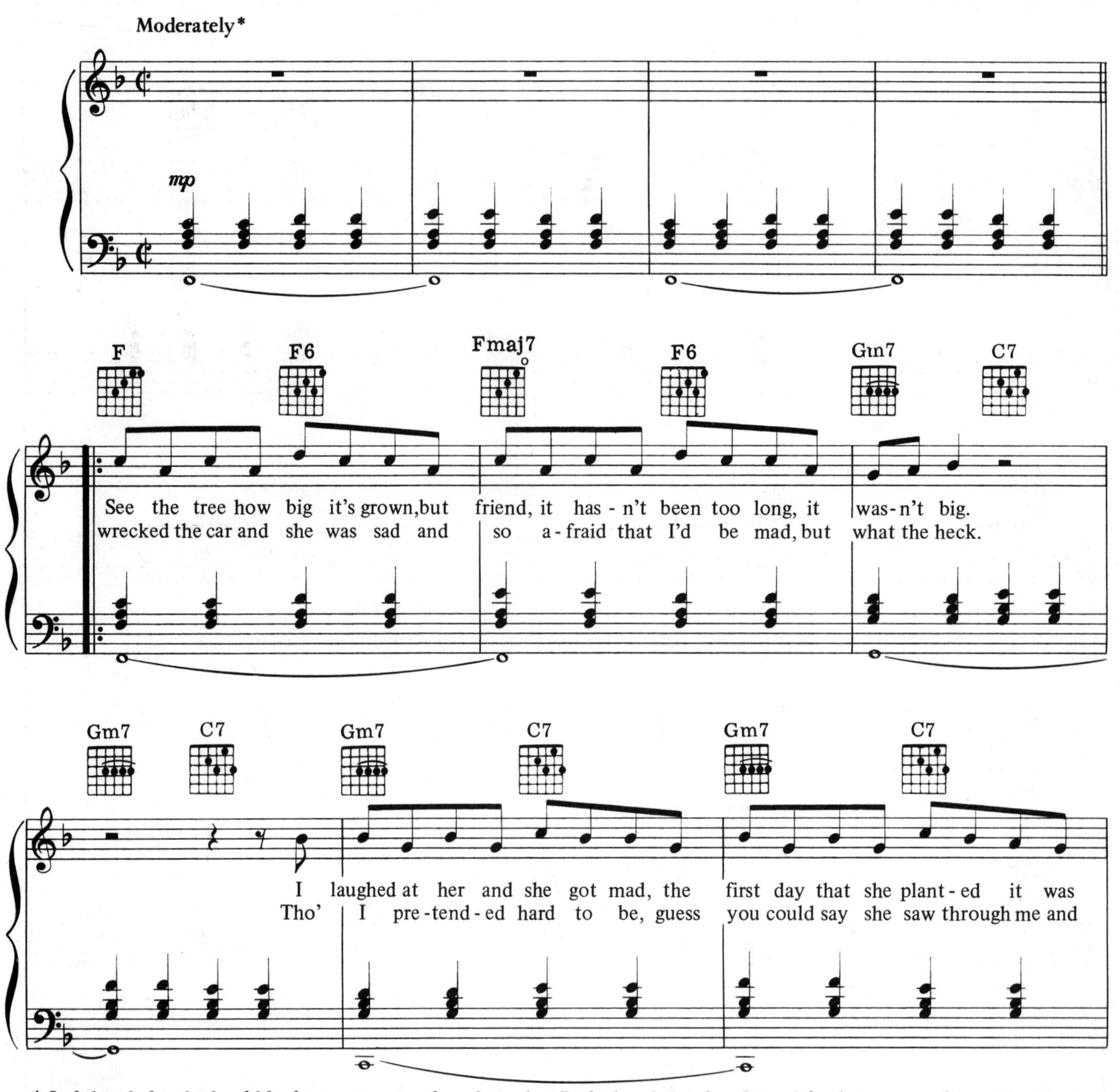

* *Left hand chords should be kept very smooth and steady. Right hand may be phrased freely, as a vocalist might sing it.*

F F6 Fmaj7 F6 F F6

just a twig. Then the first snow came and she ran
hugged my neck. I came home un - ex - pect - ed - ly and

Fmaj7 F6 Gm7 C7 Gm7 C7

out to brush the snow a - way so it would - n't die, Came
found her cry - ing need - less - ly in the mid - dle of the day, And

Gm7 C7 Gm7 C7

run - nin' in all ex - cit - ed, slipped and al - most hurt her - self, I
it was in the ear - ly Spring when flow - ers bloom and rob - ins sing she

F F6 Fmaj7 F6 F F6

laughed 'til I cried. She was al - ways young at heart,
went a - way. Yes, one day while I was - n't home while

Fmaj7 F6 Gm7 C7 Gm7 C7
kind - a dumb and kind - a smart and I loved her so.
she was there and all a - lone the an - gels came.
Now
Gm7 C7 Gm7 C7 F F6
I sur-prised her with a pup - py; kept me up all Christ-mas eve two years a - go.
all I have is mem - o - ries of Hon - ey, and I wake up nights and call her name.
Fmaj7 F6 F F6 Fmaj7 F6
And it would sure em - bar - rass her when I came home from work-ing late 'cause
Now my life's an emp - ty stage where Hon - ey lived and Hon - ey played and
Gm7 C7 Gm7 C7 Gm7 C7
I would know
love grew up.
That she'd been sit - tin' there and cry - in'
A small cloud pass - es o - ver - head and

Gm7 C7 F F6 F N. C.

o - ver some sad and sil - ly late, late show.
cries down in the flow - er bed that Hon - ey loved.

And Hon - ey, I

Gm7 C7 Gm7 C7 F F6

miss you, and I'm be - ing good.

Fmaj7 F6 Gm7 C7 Gm7 C7

And I'd love to be with you if on - ly I

1. F F6 Fmaj7 F6

could. She

2. F F6 Fmaj7 F6 F

could.

slower

LITTLE GREEN APPLES

Words and Music by
BOBBY RUSSELL

Cm
3fr
Am7
D7
And I look a - cross at smil - ing lips that
But ___ she sits wait - ing pa - tient - ly and
Am7
D7
G
Gmaj7
G6
G5
warm my heart and see my morn - ing sun.
smiles when she first sees me 'cause she's made that way.
And if that's not
Am7
D7
Am7
D7
Am7
D7
Am7
D7
lov - in' me, then all I've got to say:
G
God did - n't make lit - tle green ap - ples and it don't rain in In - dian - ap - 'lis in the
God did - n't make lit - tle green ap - ples and it don't snow in Min - ne - ap - 'lis whenthe

Am
sum-mer time.
There's no such thing as Doc-tor Suess,
win-ter comes.
There's no such thing as make be-lieve,

Dis - ney - land and Moth - er Goose is no nurs-'ry rhyme.
pup - py dogs and au - tumn leaves and B. B. guns.

G
God did-n't make lit - tle green ap - ples and it don't rain in In - dian - ap - 'lis in the

Am
sum-mer-time,
And when my-self is feel - in' low I

G
[last time, repeat this measure and fade]
think a - bout her face a - glow to ease my mind.
Am
Am maj7
Am7
D7
Am
Am maj7
Am7
D7
Some - times I call her up at home know-ing she's
G
Gmaj7
G6
G5
Am
Am maj7
bus - y
And ask if she could get a - way and
D.S. 𝄋 and fade on chorus
Am7
D7
G
Gmaj7
G6
G5
meet me and grab a bite to eat.
And

BLUE VELVET

Words and Music by
BERNIE WAYNE
LEE MORRIS

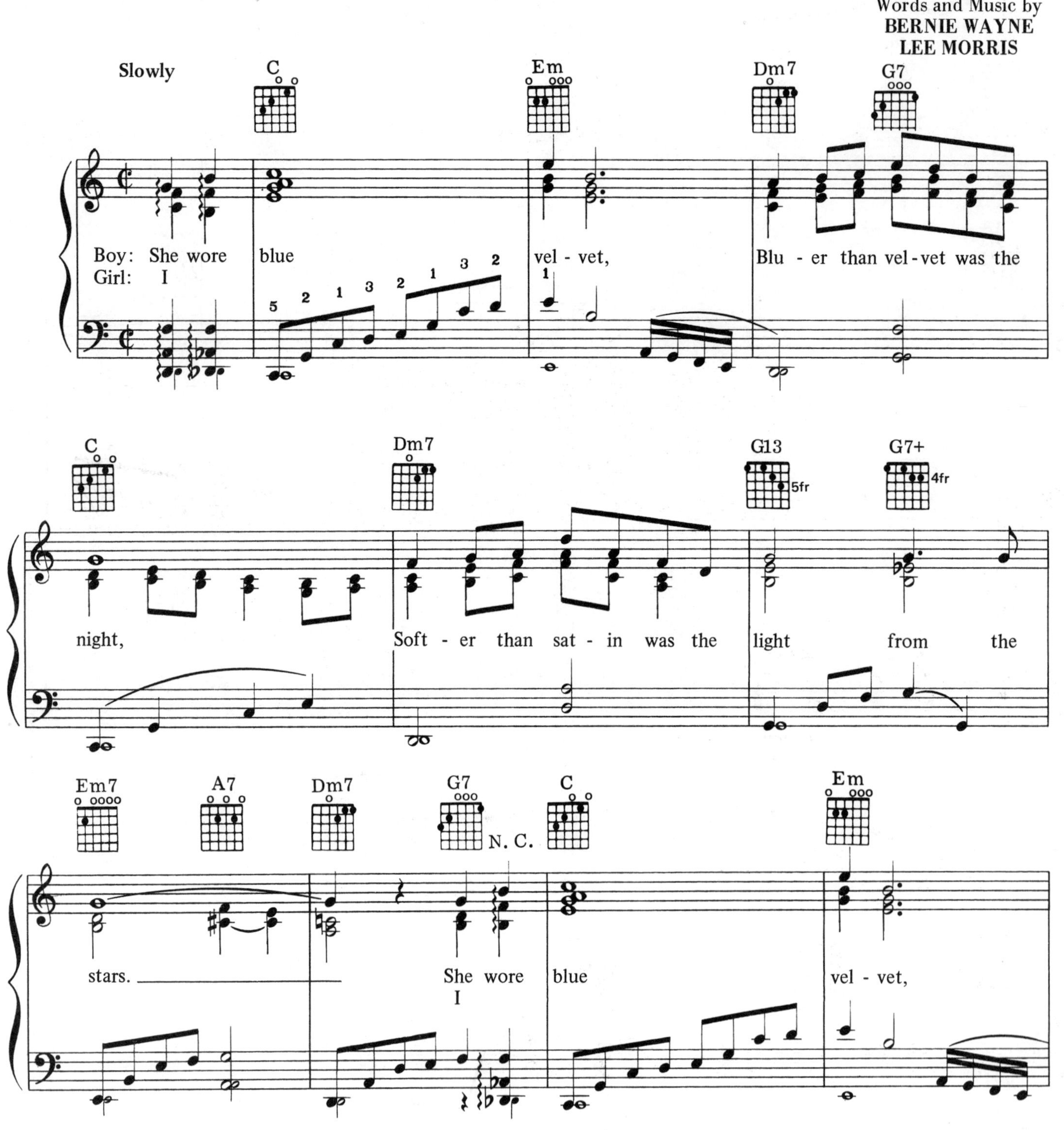

Dm7
G7
B♭7
A7
Dm7
G7
Blu - er than vel - vet were her eyes,
And as the night danced slow-ly by,
Warm - er than May her ten - der
G13
5fr
G7+
4fr
Gm7
C11
C7-9
sighs, love was ours.
5 2 1 3 2 1 3
Fmaj7
Fm7
Em7
Am7
3
Ours, a love I held tight - ly,
Feel - ing the rap - ture
C11
C7-9
Fmaj7
Fm7
grow,
Like a flame burn - ing bright - ly,

Em7
Cdim
Dm7
G13
G7+
C
But when she left, gone was the glow of blue
Em
Dm7
G7
B♭7
A7
vel - vet, But in my heart there'll al - ways be,
Dm7
G11
G7+
Gm7
Pre - cious and warm, a mem - o - ry through the years,
C11
Fmaj7
G7+
C
N. C.
And I still can see blue vel - vet through my tears.

WHEN MY BABY SMILES AT ME

Words and Music by
HARRY VON TILZER,
ANDREW B. STERLING, BILL MUNRO
and TED LEWIS

D7
dise.
And when my ba - by
smiles at me
there's such a
won - der - ful light in her
G
eyes,
Eb7 G Gdim G
The kind of light that means just

G7
7fr
F#7
6fr
F7
5fr
E7
4fr
love, the kind of love
Am
C
that brings sweet har - mon - y. I sigh, I
Eb7
G
Tacet
Am7
cry, It's just a glimpse of heav - en when my ba - by
A7
D9
G
Tacet
smiles at me.

GONNA GET ALONG WITHOUT YA NOW

Words and Music by
MILTON KELLEM

Dm7
Gm7
3fr
C9
girl
boy
in town
And ya
nev - er cared if it
got me down.
You
lost my pride,
Did - n't have much mon - ey but I
real - ly tried.
It
Fmaj7
Dm7
Gm7
had me wor - ried, al - ways
on my guard,
But ya
laughed at me
'cause I
made you hap - py when you
made me cry,
And ya
broke my heart
so I
C9
To Coda
F
tried so hard!
said good - bye!
Boom, boom,
Boom,
Melody
Am
Gm7
C7
Fmaj7
boom,
Gon - na
get a - long with - out ya now.
Boom,
Melody

F
Am
Gm7
3fr
C7
boom, Boom, boom, Gon - na get a - long with - out ya now.
Fmaj7
Am
Dm7
(Play)
Gm7
3fr
C9
D.S. al Coda
F
Am7
Gm7
3fr
C7
Fmaj7
boom, Boom, boom, Gon-na get a - long with-out ya now.
Boom,
Melody
Melody

LITTLE LADY MAKE BELIEVE

Words by
CHARLIE TOBIAS

Music by
NAT SIMON

F
Am
Gm7
C7
Dm
Am
What a pair of shoes for two ti - ny feet,
What a pair of gloves, the
B♭6
A7
B♭
B♭m6
6fr
E♭9
6fr
fin - gers don't meet,
Pos - ing in a glass, your joy is com - plete,
My
F/Abass
G9
G♭7
F
A
A6
lit - tle la - dy make be - lieve.
In your lit - tle arms the
B9
E7
B♭7
A6
A♭7
Gmaj7
A♭6
doll you en - fold,
Means the world and all to you;
But

A
A6
B9
E7
B♭7
you could nev - er love the doll that you hold
Half as much as I love
A
C7
F
Am
Gm7
C7
you, dear.
Dream your lit - tle dreams and may they come true,
Dm
Am
B♭6
A7
B♭
May the com - ing years bring hap - pi - ness too,
All my fu - ture dreams are
B♭m6
6fr
E♭9
6fr
F/Abass
6fr
G9
C9
G7
G♭maj7
F
wrapped up in you,
My lit - tle la - dy make be - lieve.

HAVE YOU LOOKED INTO YOUR HEART

Words and Music by
**T. RANDAZZO, B. WEINSTEIN
and B. BARBERIS**

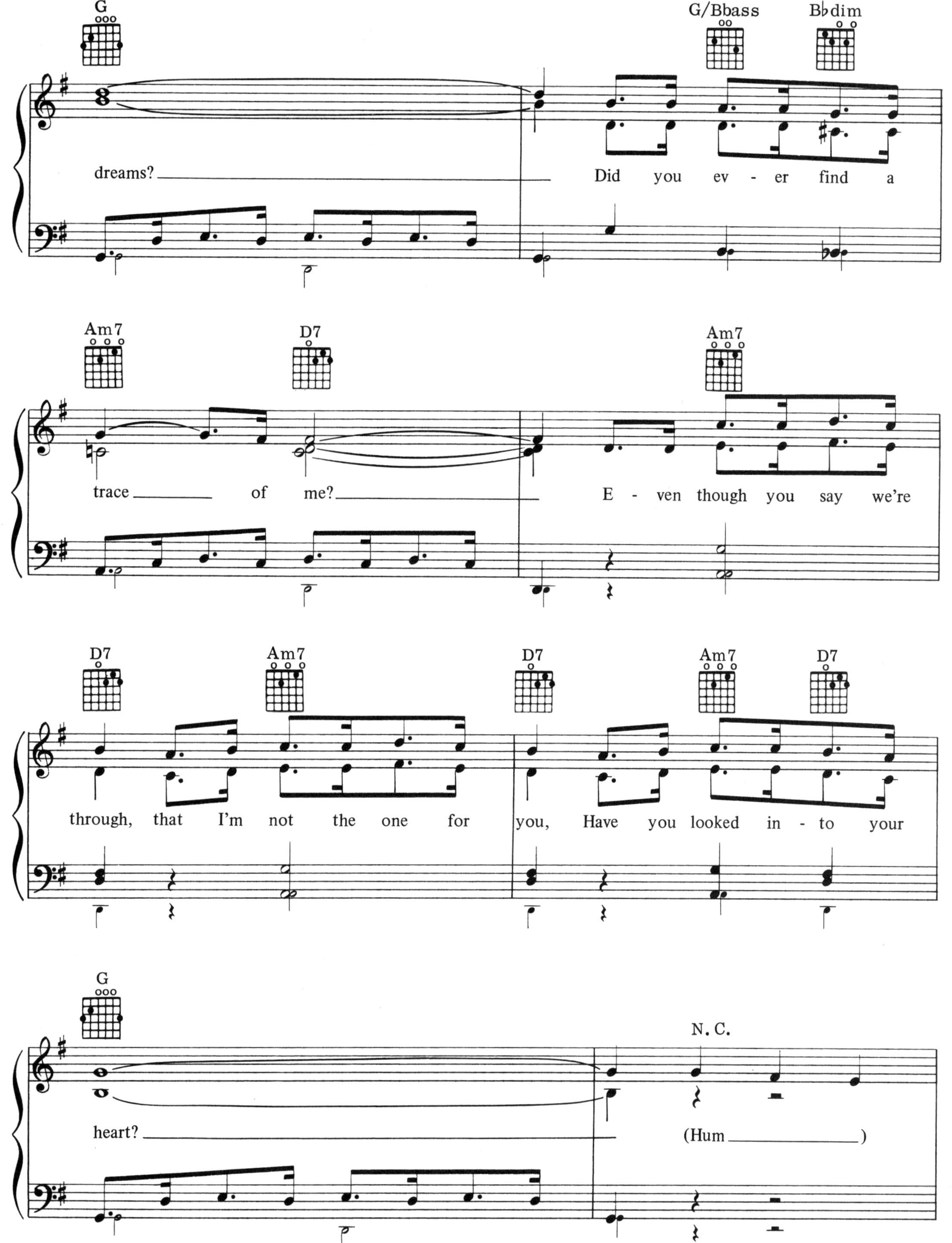
G
G/Bbass
B♭dim
dreams?
Did you ev - er find a
Am7
D7
Am7
trace of me?
E - ven though you say we're
D7
Am7
D7
Am7
D7
through, that I'm not the one for
you, Have you looked in - to your
G
N.C.
heart?
(Hum)

B7
When the eve - ning shad - ows fall up -
Em
Gaug
Em7
on my win - dow pane, I
A7
find I'm cry - ing o - ver
Cm6
D7
N. C.
o - ver and o - ver and o - ver and o - ver a - gain. Ev - er since we've been a -

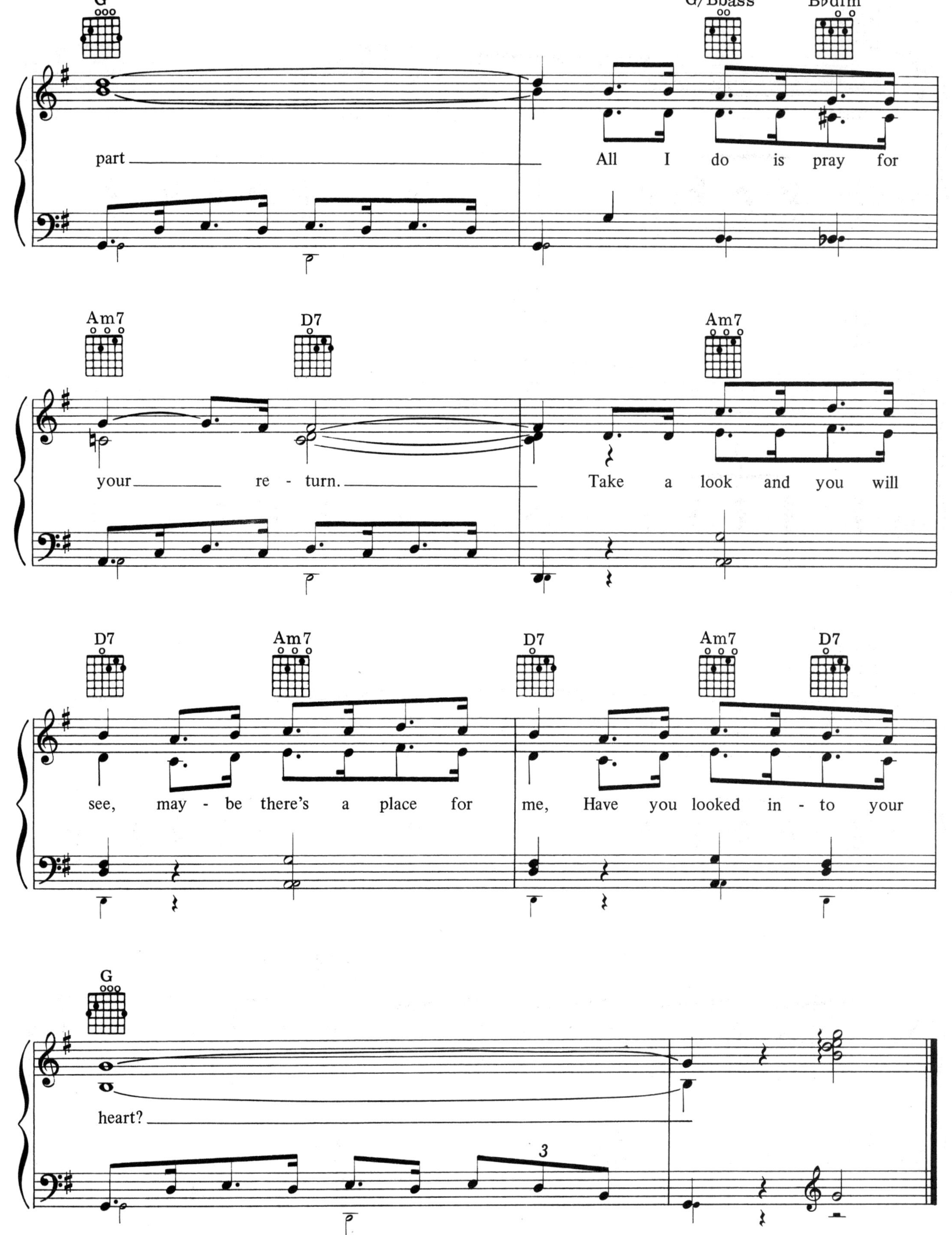
G
G/Bbass
B♭dim
part
All I do is pray for
Am7
D7
Am7
your re - turn.
Take a look and you will
D7
Am7
D7
Am7
D7
see, may - be there's a place for
me, Have you looked in - to your
G
heart?
3

THE WAYWARD WIND

Words and Music by
HERB NEWMAN
and STAN LEBOWSKY

D
A7
G
D
last time, end here
kin to the way - ward wind.
8
D
In a lone - ly shack by a rail - road track {He / I} spent {his / my} young - er
Oh I met {him there / a girl} in a bor - der town {He / I} vowed we'd nev - er
days, And I guess the sound of the out - ward bound
part, 'Tho {he / I} tried {his / my} best to set - tle down
A7
3
D
D.C.
Made {him / me} a slave to {his / my} wand' - rin' ways.
{I'm / She's} now a - lone with a brok - en heart.

TURN BACK THE HANDS OF TIME

Words and Music by
JIMMY EATON, LARRY WAGNER
and CON HAMMOND

Ab
4fr
Bb7
6fr
Eb
3fr
While I held your hand in mine Our dream came true.
If my heart could sing to-night How it would cry:
Chorus:
Eb
3fr
G7+5
G7
Ab
4fr
Bb7
6fr
D/Bbbass
Turn back the hands of time, Roll back the
Eb
3fr
Dbmaj7
C7
Fm7
Abm6
sands of time, Bring back our dream di - vine,
Eb
3fr
Ebdim
Bb7
6fr
1.
Eb
3fr
2.
Eb
3fr
Let's live it o - ver a - gain.
gain.

THAT'S HOW MUCH I LOVE YOU

By
EDDY ARNOLD
WALLY FOWLER
J. GRAYDON HALL

3. If you were a kitten with pretty glossy fur
I'd take you up and stroke you and listen to you purr,
I'd take you up and stroke you and listen to you purr
'Cause that's how much I love you, baby,
That's how much I love you.

4. If you were a tiger I'd hang around your den
And pester you, my honey, until you let me in,
And pester you, my honey, until you let me in
'Cause that's how much I love you, baby,
That's how much I love you.

5. If you were a horse-fly and I an old grey mare
I'd stand and let you bite me and never move a hair,
I'd stand and let you bite me and never move a hair
'Cause that's how much I love you, baby,
That's how much I love you.

6. If you want to marry, now let me tell you what.
We'll go and find the parson and let him tie the knot,
We'll go and find the parson and let him tie the knot
'Cause that's how much I love you, baby,
That's how much I love you. (To Final ending)

A LOVELY WAY TO SPEND AN EVENING

Words by
HAROLD ADAMSON

Music by
JIMMY McHUGH

F
Am
Dm
Gm
3fr
eve - ning,
Can't think of
an - y - one
eve - ning,
I want to
save all my nights
Bbm
C7
F
Bbm
Bb
F6
Fine
as love - ly as
you.
and spend them with
you.
Bb
Bbm
Am7
Dm7
Gm
3fr
C7
A cas - u - al stroll thru a gar - den, a kiss by a la - zy la -
F
Gm/Bb bass
A7
Dm7
G7
D.S. al Fine
C7
goon, Catch-ing a breath of moon - light, hum-ming our fav-'rite tune.

ISLE OF CAPRI

Words by
JIMMY KENNEDY

Music by
WILL GROSZ

G
C
C#dim
5fr
G/Dbass
bove.
I said, "La - dy, I'm a
rov - er,
Em7
A7
D11
G
F
Can you spare a sweet word of
love?"
She whis-pered
soft - ly, "It's best not to
a little more broadly
G
F
G
F
D7
lin - ger." And then as
I kissed her hand I could
see
She wore a
in tempo
Am
Am+5
Am7
D9
5fr
G/Dbass
D7
G
8va
plain gold-en ring on her
fin - ger;
'Twas good - bye on the Isle of Ca - pri.

THE OLD LAMPLIGHTER

Words by
CHARLES TOBIAS

Music by
NAT SIMON

Moderately

F/Cbass
C7
F
N. C.
F
F6
long, long a - go. You'd hear the pat - ter of his feet as he came
long, long a - go. Now if you look up at the sky you'll un - der -
very softly
F
F6
F
F6
to Coda
tod - dling down the street, His smile would hide a lone - ly heart you
stand the rea - son why The lit - tle stars at night are all a -
F
Gm
Gm6
see. If there were sweet - hearts in the park he'd pass a
Gm
Gm6
Gm
Gm6
lamp and leave it dark Re - mem - ber - ing the days that used to

Gm
F
F6
be. For he re - calls when dreams were new, he loved some -
F
F6
F
B♭/Dbass
C7
F
N. C.
D.S. al Coda
one who loved him too Who walks with him a - lone in mem - o - ry. He made the
Coda
F
N. C.
F
F6
glow. He turns them on when night is here, he turns them
softer and softer till the end
F
F6
F
B♭/Dbass
C7
F
8va
off when dawn is here, The lit - tle man we loved of long a - go.
slower

OL' MAN RIVER

Words by

OSCAR HAMMERSTEIN II

Music by
JEROME KERN

Slowly, but don't drag

mf

C Am C F C F

Ol' Man Riv - er, dat Ol' Man Riv - er, He must know sump - in', But

mp *simile*

C Am G7sus4 G7 G7sus4 G7

don't say noth - in', He jus' keeps roll - in', he keeps on roll - in' a -

C Dm7 C Dm7 G7 C Am

long. He don't plant 'ta - ters, He

C
F
C
Am
C
Cdim
don't plant cot - ton, An' dem dat plants 'em is soon for - got - ten; But
Dm7
G7
Dm7-5
G7
C
Fm
Ol' Man Riv - er, he jus' keeps roll - in' a - long.
C
Am6
B7
Em
G
A
B7
Em
G
A
B7
You an' me, we sweat and strain,
mf
very steady
R.H.opt.
Em
G
A
B7
Em
G
A
B7
Em
G
A
B7
Bod - y all ach - in' an' racked wid pain. "Tote dat barge!"

Em
G
A
B7
Em
G
A
B7
C/B♭bass
B♭
G
"Lift dat bale," Git a lit - tle drunk an' you land in jail.
hold back
C
Am
C
F
C
G7
Ah gits wea - ry an' sick of try - in', Ah'm tired of liv - in' an'
in tempo start p and start to build
Am
D7-5
C
Am
Dm7
G7
skeered of dy - in', But Ol' Man Riv - er, he jus' keeps roll - in' a -
f
1.
C
Fm
C Dm7-5 G7sus4 G7
long.
2.
C
F
G7
C
long.
f
con 8

BILL

Lyrics by
P. G. WODEHOUSE and
OSCAR HAMMERSTEIN II

Music by
JEROME KERN

F7 C7 F C7 F7 F7+ B♭maj7 Dm7 Gm7 G7-9
find in a sta - tue. And I can't ex - plain, it's
nat - u - ral to me. And I can't ex - plain, it's
in tempo again
Cm7 F11 F+ B♭13 E♭maj7 E♭6
sure - ly not his brain that makes me thrill. I
sure - ly not his brain that makes me thrill. I
Em7-5 C7 B♭ Edim Cm7 F7-9
2nd time only
love him be-cause he's won-der - ful, Be-cause he's just old
love him be-cause he's I don't know, be-cause he's just my
simply
1. B♭ G7 Cm F7 B♭
Bill. He's
2. B♭ Dm7 Gm7 Bdim Cm7 F7-9 B♭6add9
Bill.
L.H.
delicately

MAKE BELIEVE

Words by
OSCAR HAMMERSTEIN II

Music by
JEROME KERN

A7
lieve our lips are blend - ing in a
D
E7
3
phan - tom kiss or two or three? Might as
G6
G♯dim
D/Abass
D♯dim
well make be - lieve I love you For to
f
mp
A7
A7-9
D
Gm6
D
tell the truth I do.

WHY DO I LOVE YOU?

Words by
OSCAR HAMMERSTEIN II

Music by
JEROME KERN

G/Bbass
B♭dim
Am7
D7
You're a luck - y boy, I am luck - y too,
G
G♯dim
Am7
D7
All our dreams of joy seem to come true.
G6
G7
Cmaj7
F9
slower
May - be that's be -cause you love me,
G/Dbass
Am7
D7
E♭
3fr
Gmaj7
2fr
May - be that's why I love you.

CAN'T HELP LOVIN' DAT MAN

Words by
OSCAR HAMMERSTEIN II

Music by
JEROME KERN

Dm7
G7
Cmaj7
Gm7
C7-5-9
F6
Fm6
tell me he's slow,
Tell me I'm cra - zy,
may - be, I know,
Em7
Am7
A♭7
4fr
G7
Cmaj7
Dm7
rush it a bit
Can't help
lov - in' dat man of
mine.
Gm7
C7-9
F6
F♯dim
R.H.
L.H.
R.H.
When he goes a - way
Cmaj7
D9
5fr
Em7
E♭maj7
Dat's a rain - y day,
R.H.
L.H.
R.H.
And when he comes

Dm7
D9
5fr
G11
slower
G9
back dat day is fine, The sun will shine.
Cmaj7
in tempo
Am7
Dm7
G7
Cmaj7
Gm7 C7-5 -9
He can come home as late as can be, Home with-out him ain't
F6
Fm6
Em7
Am7
A♭7
4fr
G7
no home to me Can't help lov - in' dat man of
Cmaj7
E♭9
6fr
A♭maj7
4fr
D♭maj7
Cmaj7
mine.

SO IN LOVE

Words and Music by
COLE PORTER

D
D7-9
G
stars fill the sky, So in
C
F#7
B7sus4
B7
love with you am I.
Em
B7
E - ven without you, My
Em
Am
arms fold a - bout you, You

D
C/Dbass
Cm
3fr
know, dar - ling, why,
So in
G
Am
D7
G
love with you am I.
In
C/Gbass
D7/Gbass
G
love with the night mys - te - ri - ous,
The
mf freely
C/Gbass
D7/Gbass
G
night when you first were there,
In

C/Gbass
D7/Gbass
G
Cdim
love with my joy de - lir - i - ous
When I
Em
C7
B7sus4
B7
knew that you could care.
So
cresc.
p
mf
p
Em
B7
taunt me and hurt me, De -
Em
Am
ceive me, de - sert me.
I'm

D
D/Cbass
Bm7-5
E7
yours 'til I die, So in
get softer little by little till the end
Am7
Am7-5
G/Dbass
Gm/Dbass
love, so in love, so in
Gdim/Dbass
D7sus4
D7
love with you, my love am
G
Guitar tacet
I.

WHY WAS I BORN?

Lyrics by
OSCAR HAMMERSTEIN II

Music by
JEROME KERN

C
Cdim
G7
Dm7
G7
Why do I try
To draw you near me?
C
Am6
F
G7
Why do I cry?
You nev - er hear me?
C
Em7
Am7
D9
I'm a poor fool, but what can I do?
C
Cdim
Dm7
Dm7-5
G7
C
Eb6
Abmaj7
Dbaug11
C6
Why was I born to love you?
slower

WHAT IS THERE TO SAY

Words by
E.Y. HARBURG

Music by
VERNON DUKE

C/Ebass
D♯dim
C7
8fr
B7
7fr
B♭7
6fr
A7
5fr
giv - a - ble. You're made to mar - vel at and words to that ef -
D7/Abass
3fr
D7-5/A♭bass
3fr
G7+5
C
Dm9
Dm9/Gbass
fect, So, what is there to say and
C
D13-9
F♯m7-5
5fr
F7-5
5fr
Em7
A7-9
3
what is there to do? My heart's in a dead - lock, I'd
Dm7
Dm7/Gbass
C
Dm9
G7+5-9
4fr
Cmaj9
e - ven face wed - lock with you.
8

MY ROMANCE

Words by
LORENZ HART

Music by
RICHARD RODGERS

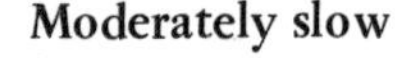

Moderately slow

C F C Am C Dm7 G7 C F C F C F♯m7-5 F7-5 Em7 Am7-5 G/Dbass D7 Dm7 G7

mp smoothly throughout

My ro-mance does-n't have to have a moon in the sky, My ro-mance does-n't need a blue la-goon stand-ing by; No month of May, no twin-kling stars, No hide a-way, no soft gui-tars. My ro-

C
F
C
mance does-n't need a cas-tle ris-ing in Spain, Nor a
Am
C
Dm7
G7
C
dance to a con-stant-ly sur-pris-ing re-frain. Wide a-
Fmaj7
Fmaj7+5 Dm/Fbass
E7+5
A7-9
D9
D7-5/A♭bass
wake I can make my most fan-tas-tic dreams come true; My ro-
C/Gbass
Am7
Dm7
G11
C
Cmaj7
mance does-n't need a thing but you.

I'VE TOLD EV'RY LITTLE STAR

Lyrics by
OSCAR HAMMERSTEIN II

Music by
JEROME KERN

G7
C
Cdim
G7
I in love? I al - ways an - swer "Yes," Might as well con -
Am
Dm7
G7
C7
F
fess, If I don't, they guess. May - be
Gm7
C11
B♭m/Fbass
Fmaj7
F♯dim
Gm7
B♭m6
F
A♭dim
you may know it too, oh, my dar - ling, if you do, Why have - n't
Gm7
C7-9
F
No chord
F
you told me?

ALL THE THINGS YOU ARE

Words by
OSCAR HAMMERSTEIN II

Music by
JEROME KERN

Gmaj7
3fr
Cmaj7
F♯m7-5
A6
7fr
Gm
F♯m
F7
star, The dear-est things I know are what you
E
Caug
Fm7
8fr
B♭m7
6fr
E♭7
4fr
are. Some day my hap-py arms will
A♭maj7
4fr
D♭maj7
6fr
G♭13
A♭maj7
4fr
B♭m11
4fr
Cm7
8fr
Bdim
6fr
(slow arpeggio)
more freely
hold you, And some day I'll know that mo-ment di - vine, When
B♭m7
6fr
E♭11
6fr
E♭7-9
5fr
(No chords)
maestoso
all the things you are, are mine.

WHO?

Lyrics by
OTTO HARBACH and
OSCAR HAMMERSTEIN II

Music by
JEROME KERN

Dreams, I know, can nev - er be true.
p cresc.
mf
D6
Em/Dbass
Ddim
D6
Seems as tho' I'll
mp cresc.
A7
G6
ev - er be blue.
Who
f
means my hap - pi - ness,

D6
Who
would I an-
mf
A7
Em7/Bbass
Cm6
A7
swer: "Yes,"
to?
mp
D
D7
Well, you ought to guess
Darned if I can guess
Who,
who,
p cresc.
G6
B♭/Dbass
D
No one but you!
f

THEY DIDN'T BELIEVE ME

Lyrics by
HERBERT REYNOLDS

Music by
JEROME KERN

Am7
D7
Bm7
eyes, your cheeks, your hair Are in a class be - yond com -
Em
Bm
F♯7
pare, You're the love - li - est girl that one could
Bm
E7
Am
see! And when I tell them,
slower
in tempo
D7
G
And I cert - n'ly am goin' to tell them,

Am
D7
That I'm the man whose wife one day you'll
G
F9
E7
Am
be They'll nev - er be - lieve me,
D7
G
Dm6
E7
No chord
They'll nev - er be - lieve me That from this
Am7
D7-9
G
great big world you've cho - sen me!

THE SONG IS YOU

Words by
OSCAR HAMMERSTEIN II

Music by
JEROME KERN

C
F9
Bb7
A7
Ab7
G7
I hear music when I touch your hand, A beau - ti - ful
Em7
Eb9
Abaug11
G7
Cmaj7
Am7
A7
mel - o - dy from some en-chant - ed land, Down deep in my heart, I hear it
Dm7
G11
G7+5
C
Am7-5
F#m7-5
E
Emaj7
say Is this the day? I a - lone have heard this
A
Dm/C
Bm7-5
B7
Emaj7
D#7
love - ly strain, I a - lone have heard this glad re - frain,

G#m 4 fr. C#9 F#7(6) C9

Must it be___ for - ev - er in - side of me,___ Why can't I let it go,___ why can't I

B7(6) F9 C/Ebass Ebdim

let you know,___ Why can't I let you know the song my heart would

Dm7 G7 Cmaj7 C9 F Bb9

sing?___ That beau - ti - ful rhap - so - dy of love and youth and spring,___ The mu - sic is

Cmaj7 Am7 A7 Dm G11 G7 C F7 Bb7 A7 Ab7 Db9 Cmaj9

sweet,___ the words are true,___ The song is you.

gradually slowing down

SMOKE GETS IN YOUR EYES

Words by
OTTO HARBACH

Music by
JEROME KERN

C
Caug
Fmaj7
F#dim
Em7
Am7
blind, When your heart's on fire, You must re - al -
Dm7
G7
C
ize Smoke gets in your eyes.
A♭
So I chaffed them and I gai - ly laughed to think they could
3
B♭m7
E♭7
A♭
doubt my love. Yet to - day My love has

C
G7
flown a - way I am with - out my love.
p
C
Em7
E♭dim
Dm7
G9
C
C aug
Now laugh - ing friends de - ride Tears I can - not hide,
Fmaj7
F♯dim
Em7
Am7
So I smile and say, "When a love - ly flame
3
Dm7
G7
G7+5
C
dies, Smoke gets in your eyes."

YESTERDAYS

Words by
OTTO HARBACH

Music by
JEROME KERN

G13-9
C9+5
C9
F9
F7-9
Gold - en days, Days of
Bb
Eb9
Dm
Gm6
A7+5-9
Dm
F7
mad ro - mance and love, Then gay youth was
with a light jazz feeling
(but subdued)
keep the left hand very smooth
Bb7
A7
Dm
F7
Bb7
A7
Dm
mine, Truth was mine, Joy - ous, free and
Dm7
Bm7-5
E7+5
A7+5-9
flam - ing life, for - sooth, was mine. Sad am
8va lower

D9+
G13-9
C9+5
F7
I,
Glad
am
I,
For
to -
B♭
E♭9
Dm
Gm6
A7+5-9
day
I'm
dream - ing
of
Yes - ter -
hold back
to 1st tempo
D6add9
G9
B♭maj7
E♭9-5
days.
D6add9
8va
L.H.
R.H.
L.H.
R.H.
Ped. al Fine
8va lower

JUNE IS BUSTIN' OUT ALL OVER

Words by
OSCAR HAMMERSTEIN II

Music by
RICHARD RODGERS

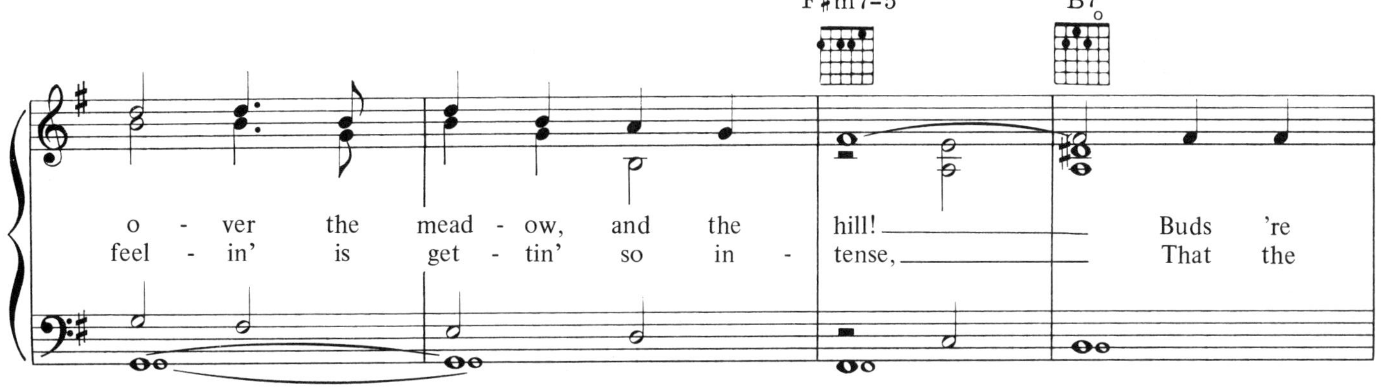

Em
Em maj7
Em7
Em6
Em-6
Em
Em7-5
bust - in' out - a bush - es And the romp - in' riv - er push - es Ev - 'ry
young Vir - gin - ia creep - ers Hev been hug - gin' the be - jeep - ers Out - a
1.
D/F♯bass
F7
Em7
A7
D11
5fr
lit - tle wheel that wheels be - side a mill!
2.
D/F♯bass
F7
Em7
A13
D11
D9
Tacet
all the morn - in' glo - ries on the fence! Be - cause it's
G
June! June, June, June!

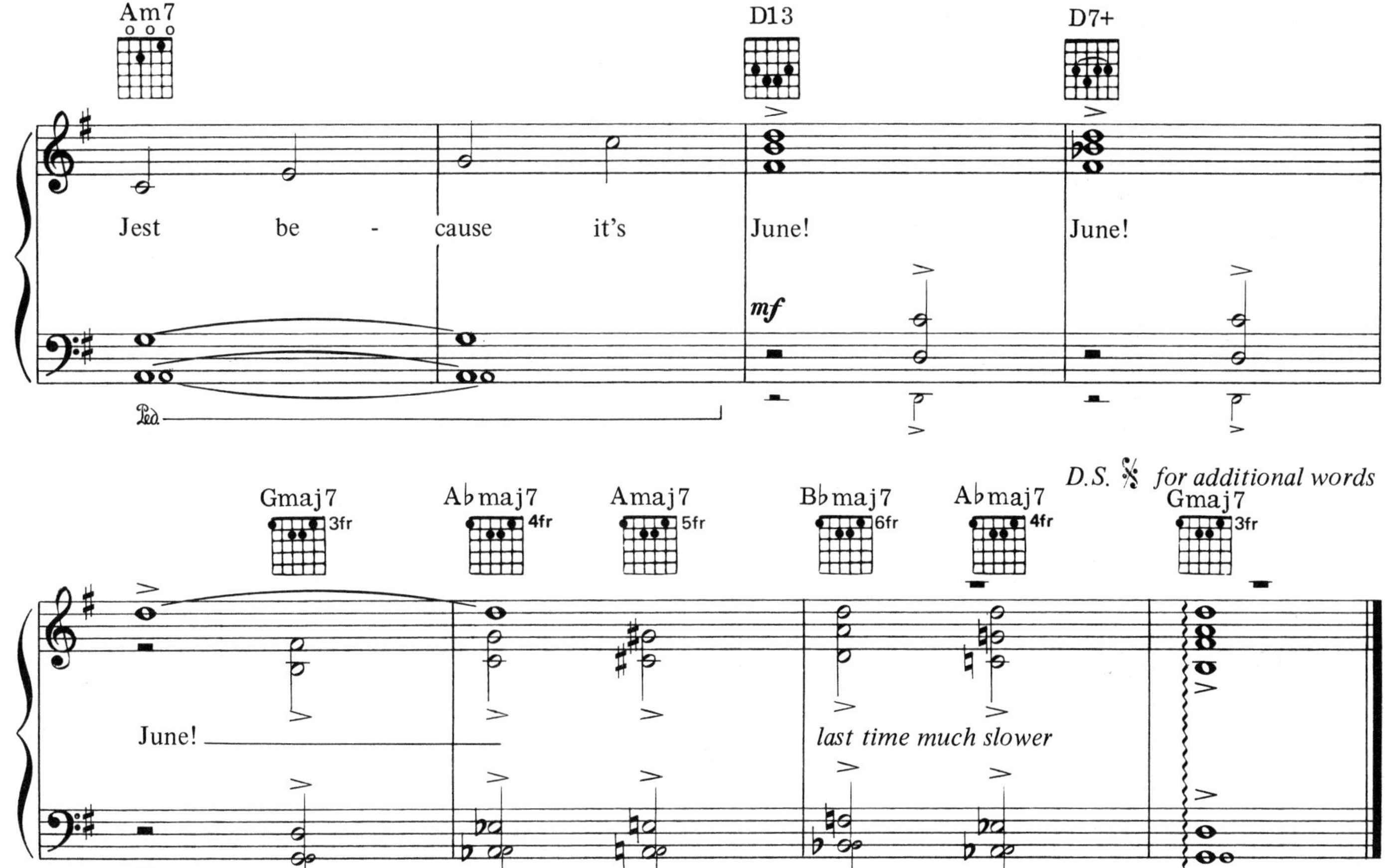

Additional Words

2. June is bustin' out all over!
The saplin's are bustin' out with sap!
Love has found my brother, Junior,
And my sister's ever lunier!
And my ma is gettin' kittenish with Pap!

June is bustin' out all over!
To ladies the men are payin' court.
Lots-a ships are kept at anchor
Jest because the Captains hanker
For a comfort they ken only get in port!

Because it's June etc.

3. June is bustin' out all over!
The ocean is full of Jacks and Jills.
With her little tail a-swishin'
Ev'ry lady fish is wishin'
That a male would come and grab her by the gills!

June is bustin' out all over!
The sheep aren't sleepin' any more!
All the rams that chase the ewe sheep
Are determined there'll be new sheep
And the ewe sheep aren't even keepin' score!

Because it's June etc.

THE MOST BEAUTIFUL GIRL IN THE WORLD

Words by
LORENZ HART

Music by
RICHARD RODGERS

Gm7
C7
bran - dy, The most beau - ti - ful girl in the
Am7
A♭maj7
4fr
5fr
Gm7
C11
world! The most
Fmaj7
E/Fbass
beau - ti - ful girl in the world Is - n't
beau - ti - ful house in the world Has a
Fmaj7
E/Fbass
Fmaj7
E/Fbass
Gar - bo, Is - n't Diet - rich But the
mort - gage, What do I care, It's good-

Gm7
C7
sweet
bye
trick
care
Who
When
can
my
make
slip - pers
me
are
be - lieve
next
it's
to
a
the
Am7-5
To Coda
D7sus4
D7
beau - ti - ful
ones that be -
world.
long.
(To Coda)
Dm9
G13-9
C
Cmaj7
So - cial?
Not a
bit!
Dm9
G13-9
C
Cmaj7
Nat - 'ral
kind of
wit,

Am7
D7
Dm7
G7
She'd shine an - y - where, And she
E♭9
6fr
D9
5fr
D♭9
4fr
C9
3fr
D.S. al Coda
has - n't got plat - i - num hair! The most
D7sus4
D7
Gm7
G♯dim
To the one and on - ly
F6/Abass
3fr
B♭9
F6/Cbass
D♭9
4fr
F6
beau - ti - ful girl in the world!

LITTLE GIRL BLUE

Words by
LORENZ HART

Music by
RICHARD RODGERS

F
Bbmaj7
C9
F
F9
8fr
F7-9
7fr
Sit there and count the rain - drops fall - ing on you.
Bb
6fr
Bbm
6fr
F
Eb7
4fr
D7
3fr
Db7
2fr
It's time you knew, all you can count on is the
Am7
5fr
Ab7
4fr
Gm7
C11
C7-9
F
Ab
4fr
G
3fr
Gb
2fr
F
Tacet
rain - drops That fall on lit - tle girl blue. No use, old
C7
F
Asus4
A7
girl, you may as well sur - ren - der, Your hope is get - ting slen - der, Why

Dm7
D7-9
4fr
Gm7
C7-9
F
Bbmaj7
C9
won't some-bod - y send a ten - der Blue boy to cheer a lit - tle girl
To Trio
F
Ab
4fr
G
3fr
Gb
2fr
Final Ending
F
Ab
4fr
G
3fr
Gb
2fr
F
blue?
blue?
Trio
Moderate waltz
When I was ver - y
mp gracefully
Gm7
C7
F
Am7
5fr
Ab7
4fr
young the world was young - er than I, As
Gm7
C7
F
mer - ry as a car - ou - sel. The cir - cus tent was

Gm7
C7
F
Am7
5fr
A♭7
4fr
strung with ev - 'ry star in the sky A -
bove the ring I loved so well.
slower
Dm7
Gm7
Now the young world has grown old,
C7
D.S. 𝄋 to Final Ending
Gone are the tin - sel and gold.

IF I LOVED YOU

Words by
OSCAR HAMMERSTEIN II

Music by
RICHARD RODGERS

Em7
E♭maj7
Dm7
D♭7
2fr
C
Cdim
know.
If I loved you,
C
Caug
Dm7
Words would-n't come in an eas - y way, 'Round in
D♯dim
C/Ebass
Eaug
Am
cir - cles I'd go.
rushing ahead
Long - in' to
Dm7
F♯m7-5
F7-5
Am/Ebass
tell you, but a - fraid and shy, I'd let my

Dm7
B♭maj7
D7
G7
C
gold - en chanc - es pass me by! Soon you'd
slowing down - - - - - - - - - to 1st tempo
Cdim
C
Caug
leave me, Off you would go in the mist of day,
Dm7
D♯dim
C/Ebass
Eaug
Nev - er, nev - er to know
rushing ahead
Dm7
Edim
Dm7
G7
C
E♭maj7
D♭maj7
3fr
Cmaj7
How I loved you, If I loved you.
much slower

WHEN YOU WERE SWEET SIXTEEN

Words and Music by
JAMES THORNTON

THE SIDEWALKS OF NEW YORK
(EAST SIDE, WEST SIDE)

Words and Music by
CHAS. B. LAWLOR and
JAMES W. BLAKE

A7
D7
G
Bridge is fall - ing down."
Boys and
D
G
C
C♯dim
girls to - geth - er,
Me and Ma - mie O' -
G
G7
C
C♯dim
G/Dbass
Rourke
Tripped the light fan - tas - tic
E7
A7
Am7
D7
G
on the side - walks of New York.

SWEET ROSIE O'GRADY

Words and Music by
MAUD NUGENT

G
D7
G
D7
And when we are mar - ried
G
D7
B7
How hap - py we'll be.
C
C#dim
G/Dbass
Em
I love sweet Ros - ie O' - Gra - dy And
A7
D7
G
Ros - ie O' - Gra - dy loves me!
Ped

IDA! SWEET AS APPLE CIDER

Words by
EDDIE LEONARD

Music by
EDDIE MUNSON

C
G7
Seems I can't live with - out you
Dm7
G7
C
Lis - ten, oh, hon - ey do.
A7
D7
I - da, I i - dol - ize ya, I
C/Gbass
D7
G7
C
love you I - da, 'deed I do.

SWEET VIOLETS

Words and Music by
J.K. EMMETT

Slow waltz

A7
D7
G
spark - ling with the dew.
Sweet
Cm6
G
C
vi - o - lets,
from moss - y dell and
Gdim
G
E7
Am
riv - u - let.
Dar - ling, dear - est
Cm6
G
D7
G
one, I plucked them and brought them to you.

ROW, ROW, ROW

Lyrics by
WILLIAM JEROME

Music by
JIMMIE V. MONACO

G6
F#7
G6
G#dim
D7/Abass
N. C.
when. He'd fool a-round and fool a-round and then they'd kiss a - gain. And then he'd
G
D7/Abass
G/Bbass
G
Am
row, row, row, A lit - tle fur - ther he would row, oh,
E7/B
Am
C
Cm6
oh, oh, oh! Then he'd drop both his oars, Take a
G/Bbass
A7
Am7
D7
G
few more en - cores, And then he'd row, row, row.

MARY'S A GRAND OLD NAME

Words and Music by
GEORGE M. COHAN

Rather freely and not fast

F/Abass
Fdim addE
6fr
5fr
C/Gbass
C7
C7+
pri - e - ty so - ci - e - ty will say Ma -
F
D7
G7
rie. But it was Ma - ry, Ma - ry,
C7
Caug
F6
E7
F6
F
A7/Ebass
D7
long be-fore the fash - ions came. And there is some-thing there that
Gm
G7
C7
F
sounds so square, It's a grand old name.

MY GAL SAL

Words and Music by
PAUL DRESSER

G7
C
C7
old
pal.
Your
trou - bles,
F
Fm6
C
Eaug
E7
sor - rows
and
care
she was
al
-
ways
will - ing
to
Am
C7
F
C
E7
A7
share.
A
wild
sort
of
dev
-
il,
but
dead
on
the
Dm
D7
G7
C
lev
-
el
was
my
gal
Sal.

I WANT A GIRL

Words by
WILLIAM DILLON

Music by
HARRY VON TILZER

C
G9
F♯9
F9
E9
good old fash - ioned girl with heart so true,
Am
E
B7
G7
One who loves no - bod - y else but you,
C
C7
F
F♯dim
D7-5
I want a girl just like the girl that
C/Gbass
Am
D9
G9
C7
Fm6
C
mar - ried dear old Dad.

GIVE MY REGARDS TO BROADWAY

Words and Music by
GEORGE M. COHAN

D7
G7
C
I will soon be there.
Whis - per of
Fm6
G7
Dm7
G7
how I'm yearn - ing to min - gle with the old - time
C
Baug
Gm/B♭bass
A7
Aaug
A7
Dm
A7/Ebass
throng.
Give my re - gards to old Broad -
Dm/Fbass
Fm6
C
Am
D7
G7
C
way and say that I'll be there ere long.

BILL BAILEY

Words and Music by
HUGHIE CANNON

F

wrong." "'mem - ber that rain - y eve - ning

F#dim

I drove you out with noth - in' but a fine tooth

Gm Bb G/Bbass F/Cbass

comb? I know I'm to blame, well ain't that a

D7 G7 C7 F

shame? Bill Bai - ley won't you please come home?"

ON THE BANKS OF THE WABASH

Words and Music by
PAUL DRESSER

WHILE STROLLING IN THE PARK

Words and Music by
ED HALEY

G/Dbass
D7
G
mo - ment my poor heart she stole a - way. Oh, a
Em
Edim
B7
No chords
sun - ny smile was all she gave to me.
B7
Em
N. C.
G/Dbass
D7
And of course we were as hap - py as could
G
D7
be. So

Moderate waltz
G
C
neat - ly I raised my hat
E7/Bbass
A7
and made a po - lite re -
D7
G
mark. I nev - er shall for - get that
C
A7
G/Dbass
D7
G
3
love - ly af - ter-noon When I met her at the foun-tain in the park.

DU, DU LIEGST MIR IM HERZEN

TRADITIONAL GERMAN SONG

G7
Du,
du
machst
mir
viel
Schmer
-
zen
C
Weisst
nicht
wie
gut
ich
dir
bin.
F
C/Ebass
G7/Dbass
C
Ja,
ja,
ja,
ja,
G7
C
D.S. optional
weisst
nicht
wie
gut
ich
dir
bin.

ACH, DU LIEBER AUGUSTIN

TRADITIONAL GERMAN SONG

Moderate waltz

A PICTURE ALBUM OF OUR TELEVISION FAMILY

A WELK PICTURE ALBUM . . .

I'd like to have you meet some members of the Welk family . . .

First, my wife, FERN . . .

This is my lovely daughter-in-law, Tanya, who is also a member of my musical "Family," as you know.

She and Larry have given me two wonderful little grandsons . . . BUNS (Lawrence Welk III)

and a fine little conductor, KEVIN PHILLIP WELK

Believe me, they keep me feeling young, in spite of . . . . . .

THE WELK MUSICAL "FAMILY" . . .

Our beautiful Champagne Lady, NORMA ZIMMER, has been a regular on our show since the New Years' Eve show at the end of 1960. Norma is active in religious work, and she has recorded quite a few beautiful inspirational albums, sometimes in duets with our friend, Jim Roberts.

JIM ROBERTS has been in the "Family" since 1955. His beautiful tenor voice never fails to give me a thrill!

This is my favorite accordion player, MYRON FLOREN. I heard Myron first in St. Louis in 1950 and hired him so I could hear him play every night. Now he is my assistant band director and a big Ranwood recording star. Myron plays every kind of music on the accordion—a versatile, wonderful musician.

Here's George Cates in action! George is our talented musical director and arranger. He was with me 25 years before I discovered he was a ham!

But speaking of hams . . . these pixillated mermaids are really two of our very pretty young singing stars, GAIL FARRELL and MARY LOU METZGER. Gail, a real Irish colleen, has been with us since 1970; Mary Lou joined us in 1973.

I'm sure you've heard her "Betty Boop" with our little band of HOTSY TOTSY BOYS. We named our little novelty gang after my own very first little band in North Dakota—before we invented our Champagne Music. From left to right we have CHARLIE PARLATO, BOB LIDO, JACK IMEL, RUSS KLEIN, DICK MALOOF, BOB HAVENS and BOB RALSTON.

A "straight" shot of Mary Lou. This young lady can sing anything from an operatic aria to an imitation of Betty Boop. She's also a fine dancer and actress.

Lucky me—surrounded by five of our lovely, talented girls. They are MARY LOU METZGER, RALNA HOVIS, NORMA ZIMMER, GAIL FARRELL and our wonderful dancer, CISSY KING.

Here's CISSY in action with her partner, BOBBY BURGESS. Bobby has been dancing with the show since 1961. He was the one who discovered Cissy for us after his first partner, Barbara Boylan, left to become a housewife. Last year, Bobby married Kristie Floren, Myron's daughter.

But Bobby and Cissy aren't the only good dancers in the "Family." Here's our Champagne Lady, Norma, with her light-footed partner.

Norma gets a lift from JOE FEENEY too!

But seriously folks, here's another really sensational dancer, our master of the taps, ARTHUR DUNCAN. Arthur once travelled to Australia for his first taste of stardom, but for the past seven years, he has been one of the Welk Family's special stars.

JACK IMEL is another expert hoofer. He's out front here with Mary Lou in a cute routine. Jack is just as lively on his marimba. In his spare time, he's assistant to Jim Hobson, producer-director of the Lawrence Welk Show.

We like to combine our talented vocal performers in duets, trios, quartets, quintets and even choruses...

DICK DALE has been with us for 20 years, since our days at the Trianon Ballroom in Chicago. He is one of our saxophonists and an all-around entertainer. Here he is singing a romantic duet with lovely GAIL FARRELL.

and in a costume number with our charming red-head, SANDI GRIFFITHS.

We call this group CURT RAMSEY'S CHAMPAGNE QUINTET. From left to right there's DICK DALE, NORMA ZIMMER, CURT, GAIL FARRELL AND CHARLIE PARLATO

This is a real-life duo, RALNA AND GUY HOVIS. Our audiences love this handsome couple, and their religious albums are always best-sellers.

A lovely looking young lady with a lovely soprano voice. This is our Mexican-born ANACANI. She's one of the newest "regulars" on the Show, and on weekends she is singing hostess at my Country Club Village restaurant in Escondido.

. . . Another member of the "Family" is handsome baritone TOM NETHERTON. We found Tom through friends in North Dakota, my home state. He's 6′5″ tall, and he's a serious fellow whose goal is to combine good entertainment with inspirational leadership.

And LARRY HOOPER has been with us since 1948! Larry joined us as a pianist, but once we got him to sing we discovered that he had a deep bass voice that drove the fans wild. This is one of my favorite pictures . . . I have just introduced Larry to the studio audience for his first appearance after his long illness. He received a standing ovation, and half the audience was crying.

JOE FEENEY is our favorite Irish tenor, by way of Nebraka. His wife Georgia is a musician, too, but these days she keeps busy with the Feeney children—all eight of them!

KEN DELO, a very warm and versatile singer, was introduced to us by Arthur Duncan, who saw him work in Australia. (He comes from Detroit.) Here he is trying out a new song on his little daughter, KIMBERLY.

Now, our country girl singer, AVA BARBER, really comes from Country Music Land—Knoxville, Tennessee. Today everyone loves country music, it seems, and everyone certainly seems to love Ava!

And now, meet some of our talented musicians . . .

This young fellow is BOB RALSTON, featured pianist and organist, and a busy recording star.

Here's Bob, playing accompaniment for "Charlie" (CHARLOTTE HARRIS), our very lovely cellist. Charlie has been with us for more than 10 years. The concert world's loss has been our gain.

JOHNNY ZELL is our trumpet star.

And HENRY CUESTA is our clarinet soloist and jazz star, successor to Pete Fountain and Peanuts Hucko.

And here's NEIL LEVANG. By the way, Neil is another North Dakota farm boy, like me.

BOB LIDO has been a favorite with our audiences for 20 years. He's a fine musician, singer and comedian. With his great personality, he was my first choice to lead the Welk Hotsy Totsy Band.

Here are some highlights from some of our favorite productions—the ones that you seemed to like too—according to the letters we received.

"ALOHA" FROM OUR 50TH STATE

BEYOND THE SEA
(LA MER)

English Lyric by
JACK LAWRENCE

Music and French Lyric by
CHARLES TRENET

F
Dm
B♭
D7
Gm
3fr
C7
Gdim
5fr
Dm
B♭
3
stands on gold - en sands And watch - es the ships that go
fly like birds on high Then straight to his arms I'd go
1.
G7
C
C7
2.
Gm7
3fr
C7
F
E7
sail - ing; Some - sail - ing. It's
A
F♯m
2fr
D6
E7
A
F♯m
2fr
D6
E7
far be - yond a star, it's near be - yond the
A
G7
C
Am
F
G7
moon, I know be - yond a
piu espr.

C
Am
Dm
G7
C
C7
Am
C7
3
doubt, my heart will lead me there soon.
dim.
We'll
p
F
Dm
B♭
C7
F
Dm
B♭
C7
3
3
meet beyond the shore, we'll kiss just as be-
F
A7
Dm
C7
F
Dm
B♭
D7
3
fore, Hap - py we'll be be-yond the sea
cresc.
Gm
3fr
C7
Gdim
5fr
Dm
B♭
G7
C7
F
3
and nev - er a - gain I'll go sail - ing.

CHANSON D'AMOUR

By
WAYNE SHANKLIN

F G9 C11
Chan - son d'A - mour Ra da da da
Chan - son d'A - mour Ra da da da
C7 Caug F A7
da, I a - dore
da, Je t'a - dore
D7 Am7-5 D7 Gm 3fr
Each time I hear Ra da da da
Chaque fois j'en - tends Ra da da da
C7 Gm7 C7 G♭7 F6 Gm7 G♭7 F6
da Chan - son d'A - mour.
da Chan - son d'A - mour.

TELL ME THAT YOU LOVE ME TONIGHT

Words by
AL SILVERMAN

Music by
C.A. BIXIO

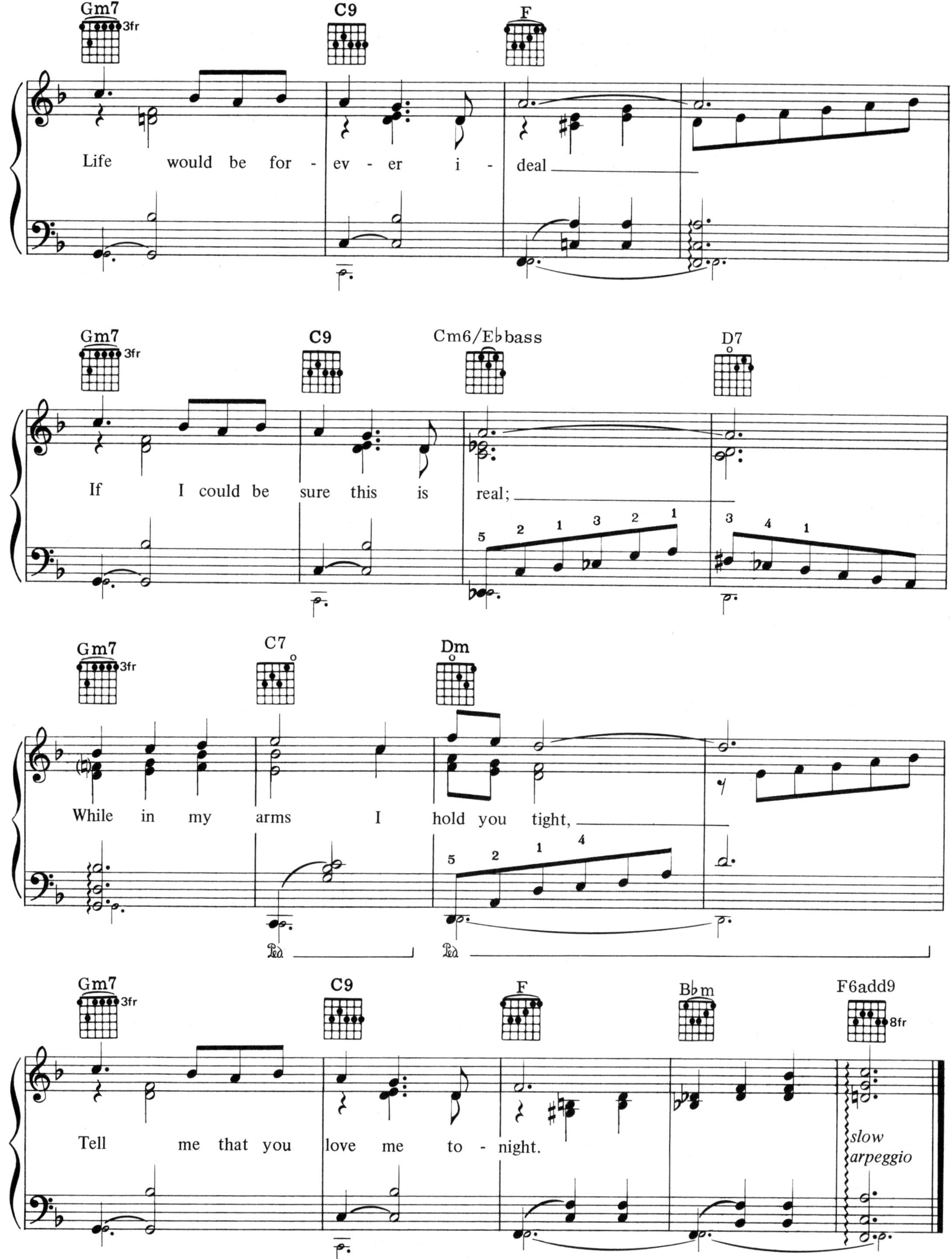
Gm7
3fr
C9
F
Life would be for - ev - er i - deal
Gm7
3fr
C9
Cm6/E♭bass
D7
If I could be sure this is real;
5 2 1 3 2 1
3 4 1
Gm7
3fr
C7
Dm
While in my arms I hold you tight,
5 2 1 4
Gm7
3fr
C9
F
B♭m
F6add9
8fr
Tell me that you love me to - night.
slow
arpeggio

ALOUETTE

TRADITIONAL

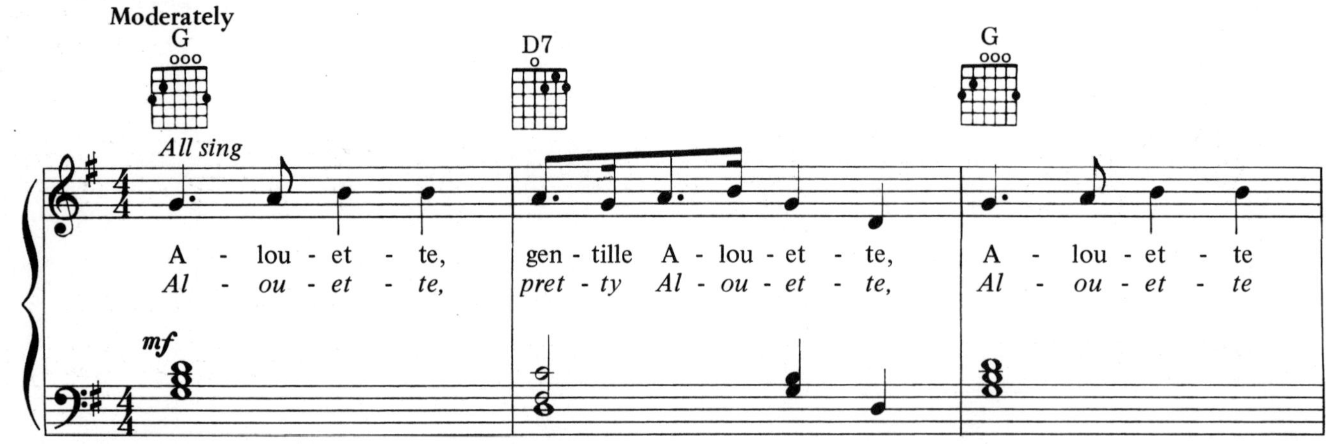

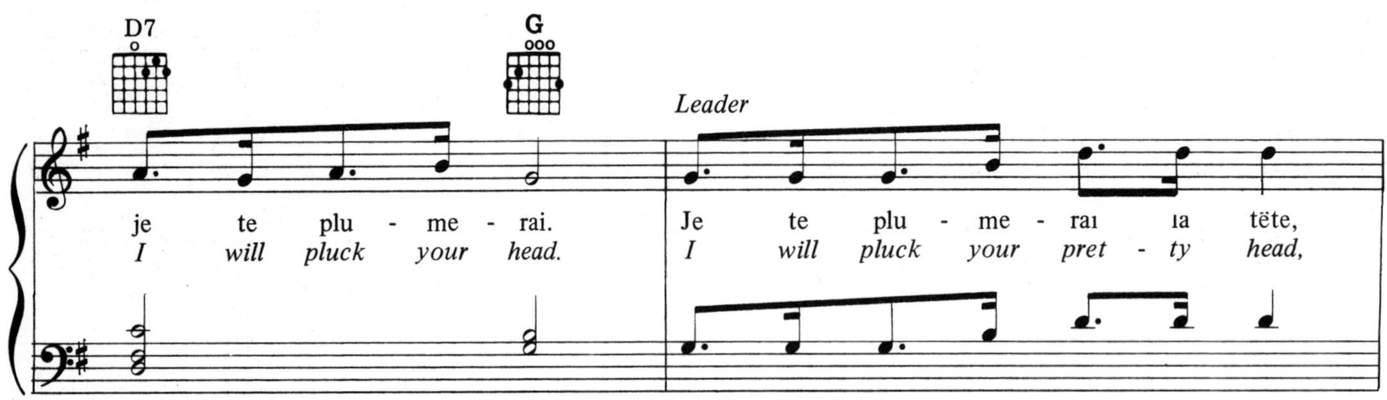

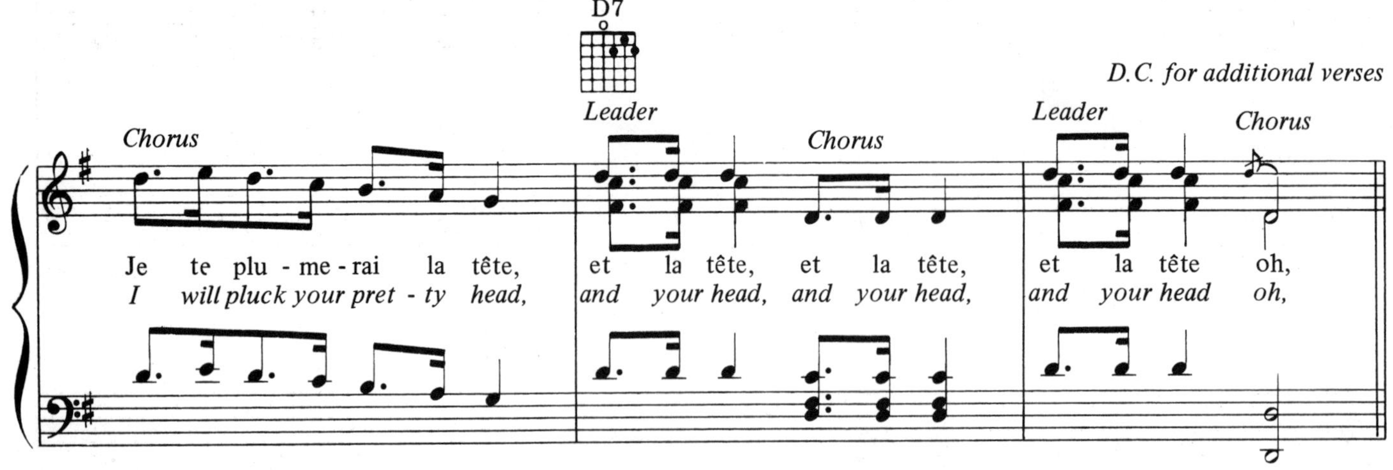

Editor's note: An alouette is a lark or skylark. Repeat each verse of this famous song adding a part of the body each time: La tête (the head), le bec (the bill), le nez (the nose), le dos (the back), Les ailes (wings), les jambes (legs), etc.

WUNDERBAR

Words and Music by
COLE PORTER

1.
2.
Fm7
bar! Wun - der -
bar! Oh I care, dear,
Bb9
Eb
3fr
Fm7
Bb9
for you mad - ly, And I long, dear, for your
Eb
3fr
Am7
D7
G
kiss. I would die, dear, for you glad - ly,
C#m7
4fr
F#7
2fr
D9(omit 3rd)
You're di - vine, dear! And you're mine, dear! Wun - der -

G
bar, wun - der - bar! There's our
fav - 'rite star a - bove, What a
D7
bright shin - ing star, Like our
G
love it's wun - der - bar!

THE SLOOP JOHN B

TRADITIONAL

Moderate Calypso beat

G
hoist up the "John B." sails,
see how the main - sail sets,
D7
send for the cap - tain a - shore,
let_ me go home.
Sher - iff John
G
Stone
let_ me go
C
home,
I
G
feel so break_ up
D7
I want_ to go
G
home.

LITTLE BROWN JUG POLKA

TRADITIONAL

G
C
D7
G
Ha, ha, ha, you and me, "Lit - tle Brown Jug" don't I love thee!
C
D7
G
last time end here
Ha, ha, ha, you and me, "Lit - tle Brown Jug" don't I love thee!
Trio
C
F
G7
C
F
G7
C
G7
C
D.C.

SKIP TO MY LOU POLKA

TRADITIONAL

Chorus:

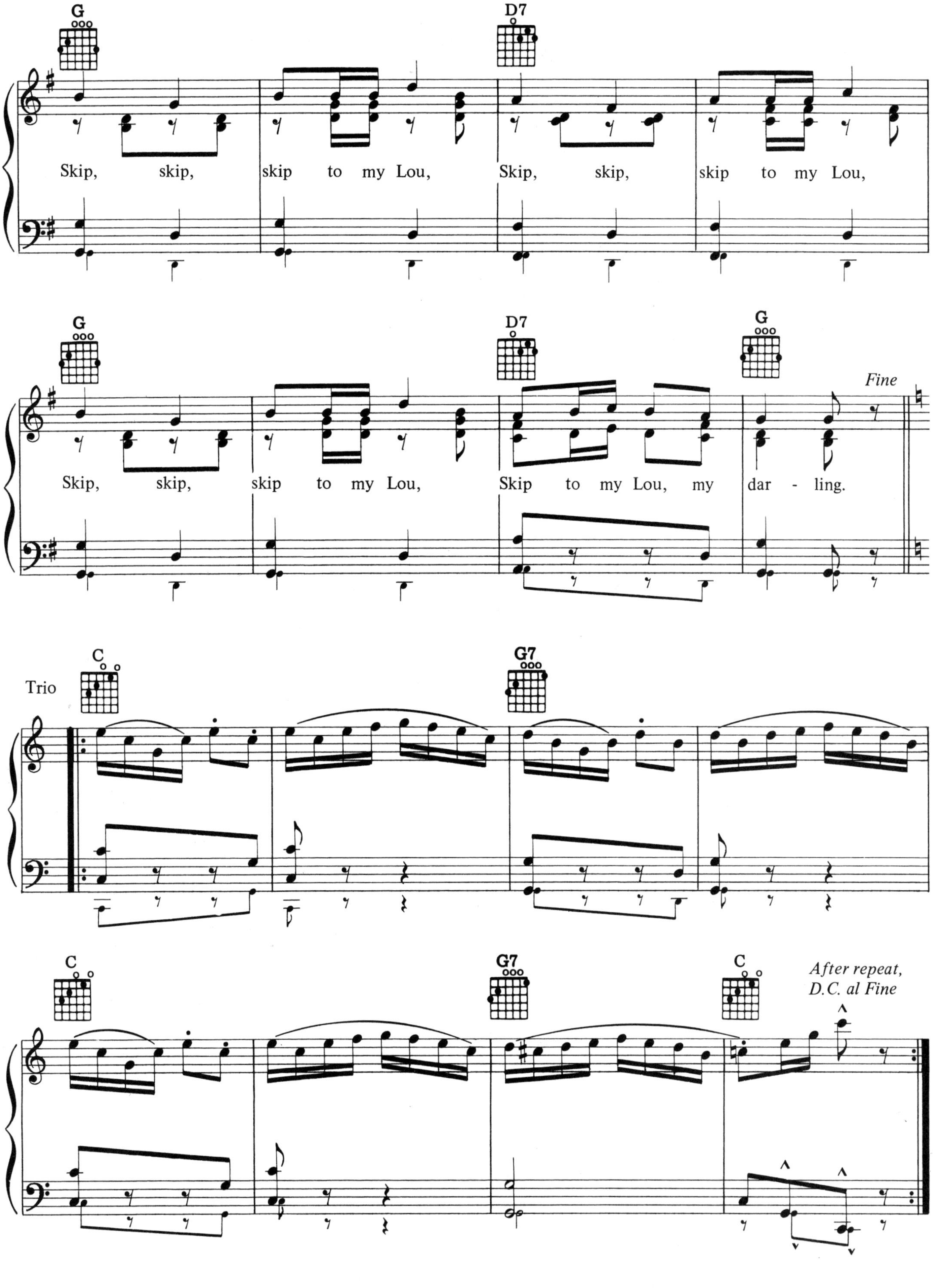

G D7

Skip, skip, skip to my Lou, Skip, skip, skip to my Lou,

G D7 G *Fine*

Skip, skip, skip to my Lou, Skip to my Lou, my dar - ling.

Trio

C G7

C G7 C *After repeat, D.C. al Fine*

SANTA LUCIA

ITALIAN FOLK SONG

O SOLE MIO

English Words by
KADISH MILLET

NEAPOLITAN SONG

ALOHA OE

By Queen LYDIA KAMEKEHA LILIUKALANI

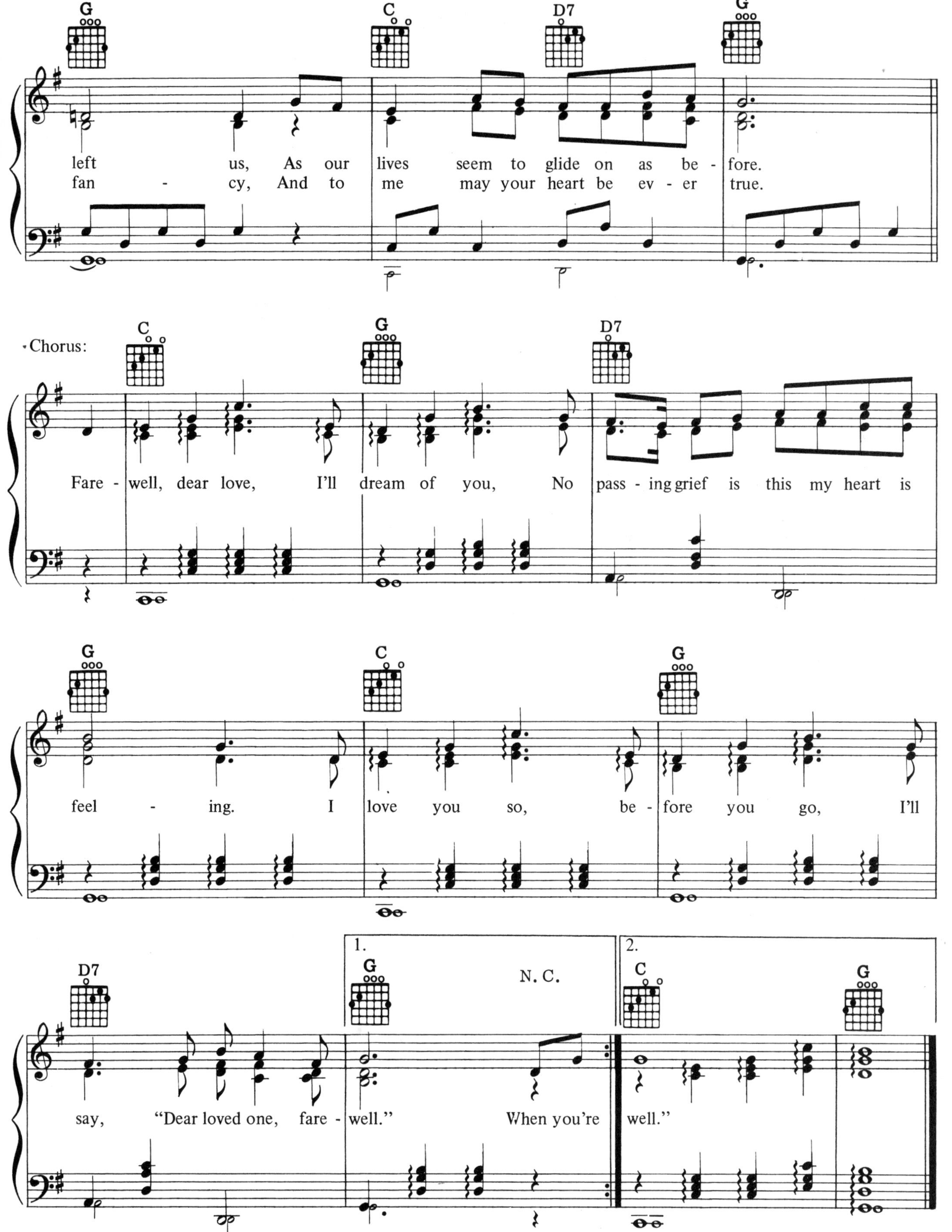
G
C
D7
G
left us, As our lives seem to glide on as be - fore.
fan - cy, And to me may your heart be ev - er true.
Chorus:
C
G
D7
Fare - well, dear love, I'll dream of you, No pass - ing grief is this my heart is
G
C
G
feel - ing. I love you so, be - fore you go, I'll
D7
1.
G
N. C.
2.
C
G
say, "Dear loved one, fare - well." When you're well."

THE WAVES OF WAIKIKI

Words by
NEAL BUHLER

Music by
ARMANDO FENNEVESSEY

C
G7
beam - ing, up - on the friend - ly sands of Wai - ki -
C
A7
Dm
ki. And once a - gain I'm dream - ing of
G7
C7
all that love - ly is - land means to me. Now
F
D7
G7
in my lone - ly bed I still see Dia - mond Head, It

C7
F
smiles up - on the beach at Wai - ki - ki. The
D7
G7
mem - o - ries I keep as I drift off to sleep Are
slow arp.
C7
F
Fdim
L.H.
ech - oes of the waves of Wai - ki - ki, Are
C7
F
B♭
F
ech - oes of the waves of Wai - ki - ki.
much slower

CINCO ROBLES
(FIVE OAKS)

Lyric by
LARRY SULLIVAN

Music by
DOROTHY WRIGHT

D
D7
G
day.
One hill I'll think of your
D
Em7
A7
laugh - ter,
One hill your cour - age in
D
D7
G
pain,
One for your beau - ty kind - ness and
D
Dm/Fbass
A/Ebass
E7
3
one for your smile,
And the last hill to hold you a -

Em7 A7 D
gain. Cin - co ro - bles, cin - co cer - os, my
A7 D
dar - ling, Five oaks and five hills a - part.
D7 G
Cin - co ro - bles, cin - co cer - os, I'll count them
A7 D G D
As each brings me near - er your heart.
3

LOCH LOMOND

TRADITIONAL

* *hillsides*

C
Am
Am/D
G5
C
G
D7
G
ev - er wont to be, On the bon - nie, bon - nie banks of Loch Lo - mond.
N. C.
G5
Oh, you take the high road and I'll take the low road, And
C
D7
Em
Bm
I'll be in Scot - land be - fore you. But me and my true love will
C
Am
Am/D
G5
C
G
D7
G
nev - er meet a - gain On the bon - nie, bon - nie banks of Loch Lo - mond.

I'M OLD FASHIONED

Words by
JOHNNY MERCER

Music by
JEROME KERN

Liltingly

F C7sus4 C7 F Fmaj7 C9 C11 F

I'm old fash - ioned, I love the moon - light, I love the

mf in tempo

C/Fbass F6 Gm6 A7 Am7 Dm7 G7

old fash - ioned things: The sound of rain up -

Dm7 D7 Gm7 Gm A♭dim

on a win - dow pane, The star - ry song that A - pril

F/A♭bass A♭13 6fr D♭maj7 C7-5 F6 Gm7 C9 Fmaj7

sings. *(no breath!)* This year's fan - cies are pass - ing

E7sus4
Bb7-5
A
E7
A
D7
E7
Adim
fan - cies, But sigh - ing sighs, hold - ing hands These my heart
Gm7
C7
F
C7sus4
C7
F
8va
un - der - stands. I'm old fash - ioned, but I don't
hold back a bit
in tempo
Fmaj7
C7
Am7
F
Bbmaj7
Bbdim
Am7
Dm7
mind it, That's how I want to be, As long as you a -
G9
F/Cbass
C7sus4
C7
F
Fmaj7
gree to stay old fash - ioned with me.

LONG AGO AND FAR AWAY

Lyrics by
IRA GERSHWIN

Music by
JEROME KERN

1.
Ab 4 fr.
Fm7
Bbm7
Eb9
Abmaj7
G7
Long the skies were o - ver - cast, But now the clouds have
C
Bb
C
C11
C6
C11
passed: you're here at last!
2.
F9
Cm7
F7 Bbmaj7
Eb9
Just one look and then I knew That all I
F6 Abdim Gm7 C7 F6 Abdim Gm7 C7 F6add9
longed for, long a - go, was you.
Ped.

DEARLY BELOVED

Lyrics by
JOHNNY MERCER

Music by
JEROME KERN

G11
Noth - ing could save me, fate gave me a sign;
same tempo as before
8va lower till *
I know that I'll be yours come show - er or shine.
*
C
D7
G11
So I say
rush a bit
mere - ly,
slowing to
original tempo
Dear - ly be -
8va lower
Ab
4fr
Gb
Eb7
Db7
Cmaj7
lov - ed be mine.
rush as before
Ped

LOVELY TO LOOK AT

Lyrics by
DOROTHY FIELDS
and JIMMY McHUGH

Music by
JEROME KERN

Gm7
C9
F
3
ag - ine find - ing a dream like you! You're love - ly to look at, it's
Dm6
E7
3
thrill - ing to hold you ter - ri - bly tight, For
C7
3
we're to - geth - er, the moon is new, And Oh, it's love - ly to look at you to -
F6
Abdim
Gm7
C7-9
F6
night!
slowing . . . .

I WILL WAIT FOR YOU

English Words by
NORMAN GIMBEL

Music by
MICHEL LEGRAND

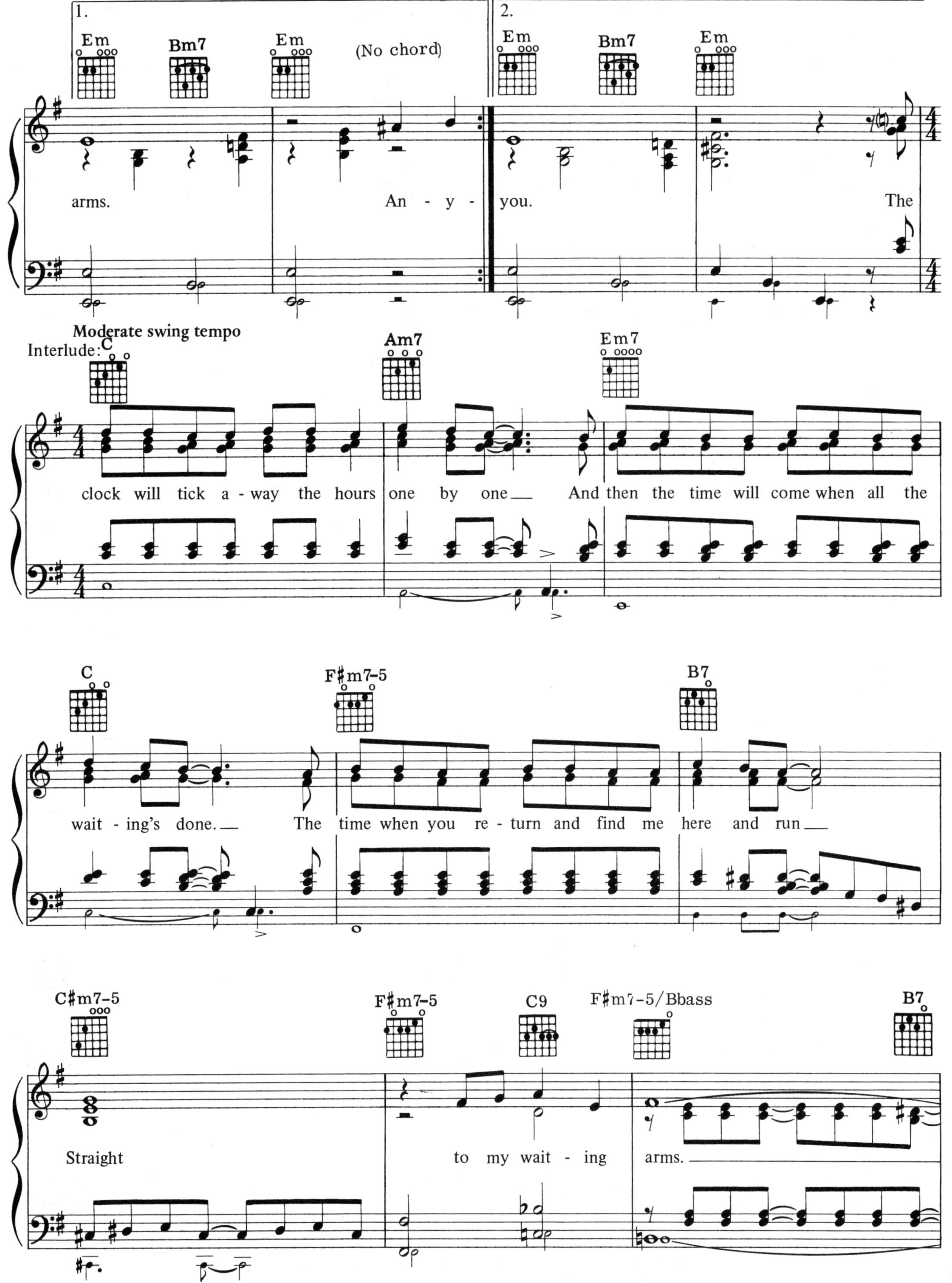
1.
Em
Bm7
Em
(No chord)
2.
Em
Bm7
Em
arms.
An - y -
you.
The
Moderate swing tempo
Interlude:
C
Am7
Em7
clock will tick a - way the hours one by one And then the time will come when all the
C
F♯m7-5
B7
wait - ing's done. The time when you re - turn and find me here and run
C♯m7-5
F♯m7-5
C9
F♯m7-5/Bbass
B7
Straight to my wait - ing arms.

Tempo I
(No chord)
Em
E7
Am
If it takes for - ev - er I will wait for you, For a
Am7
D7
Am7
D7
G
F♯m7-5
C7
B7
thou - sand sum - mers I will wait for you, 'Til you're
Em
E7
Am
F♯m7-5
here be - side me, 'til I'm touch - ing you And for -
Em
F♯m7-5
B7
Em
Bm7
Em
ev - er more shar - ing your love.

CARIOCA

Lyrics by
EDWARD ELISCU
and GUS KAHN

Music by
VINCENT YOUMANS

Moderate Latin beat

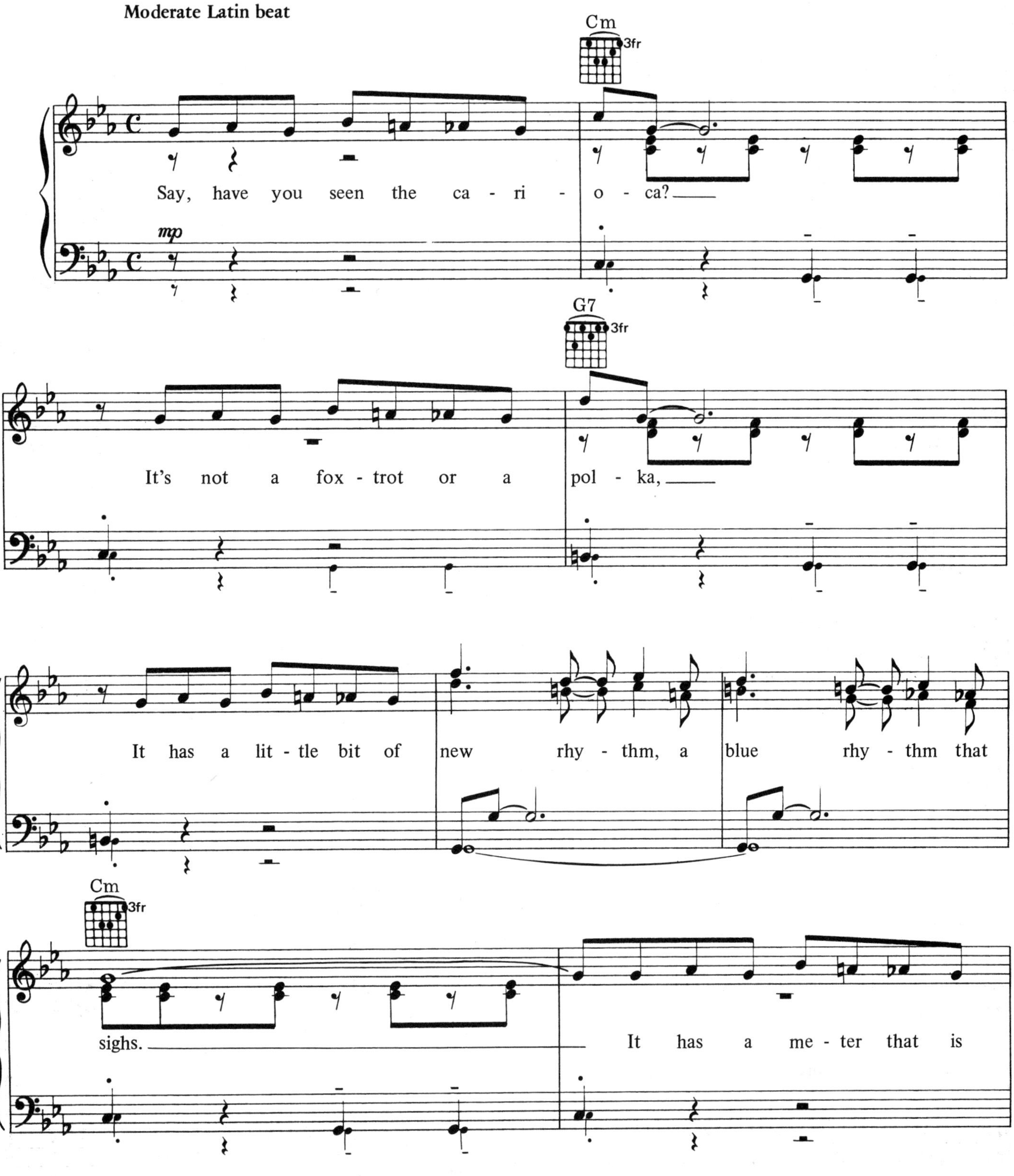
Cm
3fr
Say, have you seen the ca - ri - o - ca?
mp
G7
3fr
It's not a fox - trot or a pol - ka,
It has a lit - tle bit of new rhy - thm, a blue rhy - thm that
Cm
3fr
sighs.
It has a me - ter that is

trick - y,
A bit of wick - ed, wack - i -
G7
3fr
wick - y.
But when you dance it with a
C
new love there'll be true love in her eyes.
You'll dream of the new ca - ri -

G7
o - ca, Its theme is a kiss and a
C
sigh. You'll dream of the new ca - ri -
G7
o - ca, When mu - sic and lights are gone
C
and we're say - ing good - bye.

THE LAST TIME I SAW PARIS

Words by
OSCAR HAMMERSTEIN II

Music by
JEROME KERN

Am7 D7 G

ev - 'ry street ca - fe. The last time I saw Par - is, Her

D7 Cm D7

trees were dressed for spring, And lov - ers walked be - neath those trees, And

Am7 D11 5fr D7-9 G G/Abass A7 D

8va

birds found songs to sing. I dodged the same old tax - i - cabs that

a little brighter

G/Abass A7 D7 A/Bbass B7 E

I had dodged for years; The cho - rus of their squeak - y horns was

* *G♯ and G♮ together.*

Am7
D11
5fr
D7
G
mu - sic to my ears. The last time I saw Par - is, Her
slower
in tempo, but a little more deliberately
D7
Am7
D11
5fr
D7-9
heart was warm and gay. No mat - ter how they
Dm6
E7sus4
E7
Am7
D7-9
3
change her I'll re - mem - ber her that
G6
No chords
way.
speeding up
Repeat as often as desired. Fade out gradually.

YOU COULDN'T BE CUTER

Lyrics by
DOROTHY FIELDS

Music by
JEROME KERN

fresh from the clean - er, You are the lit - tle grand slam I'll
Am7
D7
G
G7
C
bring to my fam - i - ly. My ma will show you an
Cm
G/B bass
al - bum of me that - 'll bore you to tears! And
C
Cm
G/Bbass
E♭7/B♭bass
Am7
D7
you'll at - tract all the rel - a - tives we have dodged for years and years. And

G
what - 'll they tell me?
Ex - act - ly, what - 'll they tell me?
Gmaj7
G6
Am7
D7
They'll say you could - n't be nic - er, could - n't be sweet - er,
crescendo to the end
Bm7
Em7
Cmaj7
Am7
Bm7
E7-9
Am7
D7
could - n't be bet - ter, could - n't be smooth - er, could - n't be cut - er ba - by than you
1.
G
D7
are!
You
2.
G
are!

THE WAY YOU LOOK TONIGHT

Words by
DOROTHY FIELDS

Music by
JEROME KERN

Dmaj9
Bm7
Em7
A9
Dmaj9
Bm7
Em
A7
night.
Oh, but you're
Dmaj9
Bm7
Em7
A11
A7-9
love - ly,
with your smile so warm
D
B11
B7-9
Em7
A7
And your cheek so soft,
There is noth - ing
for me but to
D11
5fr
Ab7-5
G
C9aug11
A7-9
love you
Just the way you
look to -

Dmaj9 Bm7 Em7 A9 Dmaj9 Bm7 B♭m maj7 C7-9
night.
F Am7-5 D7-9 Gm7 C11 C7-9 F Am7
With each word your ten - der - ness grows, tear - ing my fear
more broadly
A♭13 C11 C7 F A♭maj7 A♭7
a - part, And that laugh that
Gm7 C9 C7-9 Fmaj7 F B♭9 Gm6/Abass A7-9
wrink - les your nose touch - es my fool - ish heart.

Dmaj9
Bm7
Em7
A11
A7-9
D9
C9
Love - ly, nev - er, nev - er change, Keep that breath-less
B11
B7-9
Em7
A7
D11
5fr
A♭7-5
charm, Won't you please ar - range it, 'cause I love you,
G
C9aug11
A7-9
Dmaj9
Bm7
Em7
A9
Dmaj9
Bm7
Just the way you look to - night, mm mm mm
Em7
A9
G
C9aug11
A7-9
D6
mm Just the way you look to - night.
p
pp
8va

WATCH WHAT HAPPENS

English words by
NORMAN GIMBEL

Music by
MICHEL LEGRAND

Fmaj7
Gb maj7
Gmaj7
Gb maj7
F
watch what hap - pens. One some - one who can look in your
G7
Dm7
G7
Gm7
C7
Gm7
C7
eyes and see in - to your heart, Let him find you and
Fmaj7
Gb maj7
Gmaj7
D.C. al Coda
Ab maj7
watch what hap - pens.
Coda
F6
Gb 6
E6
see; Let some-one give his
F6
Gb 6
E6
Fmaj7
F6
Fmaj7
F6
Fmaj7
heart, Some - one who cares like me.

PICK YOURSELF UP

Lyrics by
DOROTHY FIELDS

Music by
JEROME KERN

Dmaj7
D6
Bm7
E7
Am7
D7
pick your - self up, dust your - self off, start all o - ver a -
G
Abmaj7
Ab6
Abmaj7
Ab6
gain. Work like a soul in - spired till the
N. C.
Eb7
Ab
4fr
Ab6
Ab7
C
bat - tle of the day is won. You may be sick and
Am7
D9
Gm7
C11
tired, but you'll be a man, my son!

Gm7
C7
Fmaj7
B♭maj7
Em7-5
A7
Will you re-mem-ber the fa-mous men who had to fall to
Dm7
G7
Cmaj7
C7
C6
Caug
rise a-gain? So take a deep breath,
Am
Am maj7
Am7
Am6
Gm
Gm maj7
pick your-self up, dust your-self off,
Gm7
Gm6
C11
C7
F
start all o-ver a-gain.

THE TENNESSEE WIG-WALK

Words by
NORMAN GIMBEL

Music by
LARRY COLEMAN

Bb
F
Bb
F
toes to-geth-er, your knees a - part, bend your back, get read - y and start.
mf
p
Bb
F
Dm
Flap your el - bows just for luck then wig - gle and wad - dle like a
mf
mp
Bb
F
F
ba - by duck.
Won't you dance with me, hon - ey, Tap your
Oh, I love you my hon - ey, Won't you
mp
Bb
F
Dm
toes and glide,
be my bride,
and we'll al - ways be to - geth - er
mp

G7
C7
F
side by side. We'll walk with a wig - gle and a
Bb
F
G7
C7
F
gig - gle and a squawk do - in' the Ten - nes - see wig - walk.
f
Bb
F
Walk with a wig - gle, wig - gle with a walk and you're
mf
mp
G7
1C7
F
2C7
F
do - in' the Ten - nes - see wig - walk. Put your wig - walk.
f
mp
f

WILDWOOD FLOWER

TRADITIONAL

Brightly

C F C G C

mf

I will twine thru my tress - es of ra - ven black hair
Oh, he taught me to love him, he called me his flow'r
Oh, I'll dance and I'll sing and my heart will be gay

F C G C

With the ros - es so red and the lil - ies so fair,
A bright blos - som to cheer him thru life's wea - ry hour,
I'll ban - ish this weep - ing, drive trou - bles a - way,

F C

With the myr - tle as bright as the em - er - ald dew, The
Yes, but now he is gone and he's left me a - lone The
But I'll live yet to see that he'll rue this dark hour When he

G C

D.C.

ghost - ly pale rid - er with eyes of__ bright blue.
wild - flow'ers to weep and the wild birds to mourn.
won and ne - glect - ed this frail wild - wood flow'r.

WABASH CANNONBALL

TRADITIONAL

SHE'LL BE COMIN' 'ROUND THE MOUNTAIN

TRADITIONAL

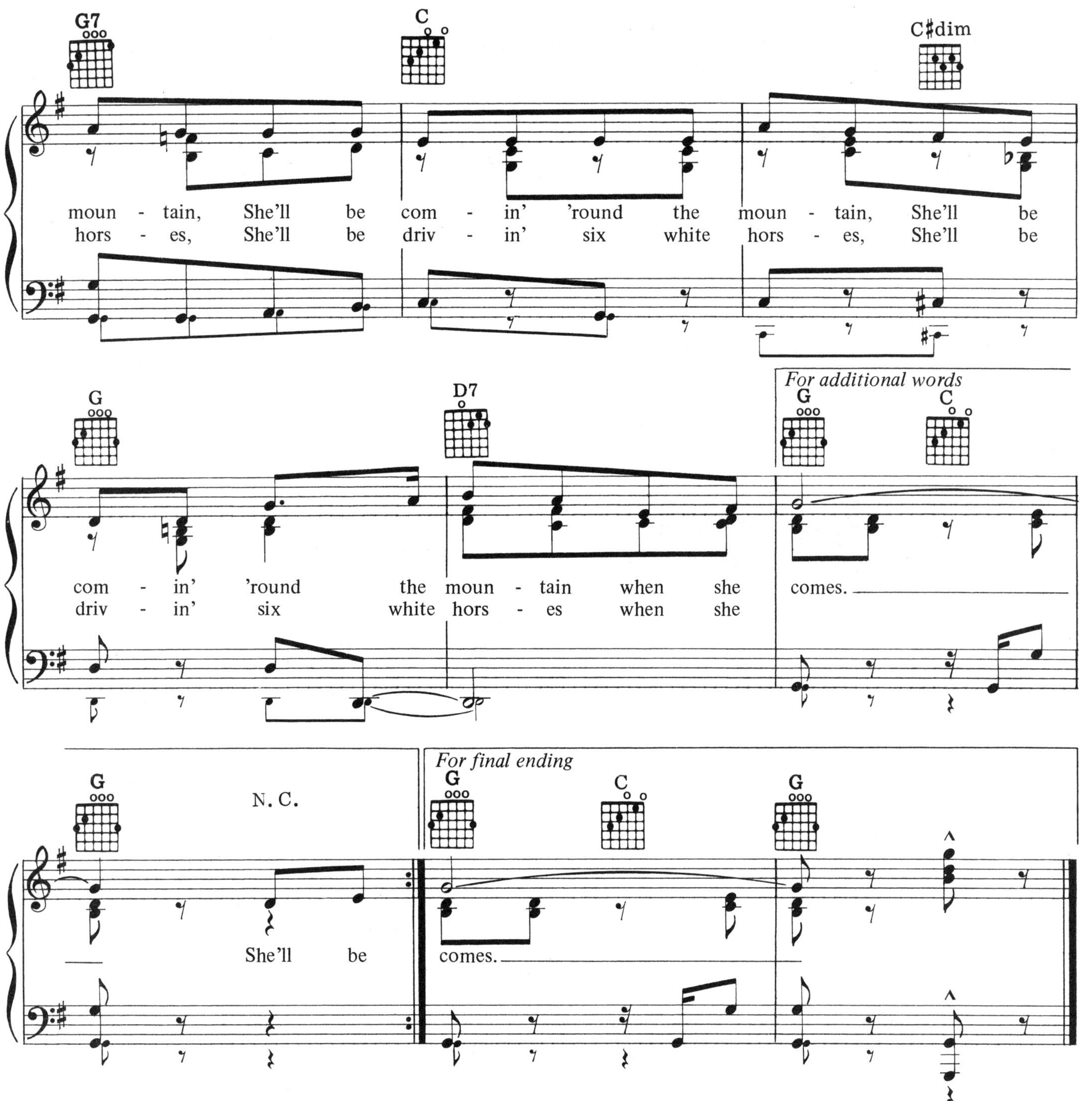

Additional Words

3. She'll be wearin' red pyjamas when she comes...
4. We will all go down to meet her when she comes...
5. We'll be singin' hallelujah when she comes...

PISTOL PACKIN' MAMA

Words and Music by
AL. DEXTER

Moderate Blues Tempo

Additional Words

3. Drinkin' beer in a cabaret
And dancing with a blonde,
Until one night she shot out the light,
Bang! That blonde was gone.
(Chorus)

4. I'll see you ev'ry night, Babe,
I'll woo you ev'ry day,
I'll be your regular daddy
If you'll put that gun away.
(Chorus)

5. Drinkin' beer in a cabaret,
And was I havin' fun!
Until one night she caught me right
And now I'm on the run.
(Chorus)

6. Now there was old Al Dexter,
He always had his fun,
But with some lead, she shot him dead
His honkin' days are done.
(Chorus to last ending)

THE YELLOW ROSE OF TEXAS

TRADITIONAL

Brightly, with spirit

Chorus:
C
G
She's the sweet - est rose of col - or this fel - low ev - er
A7
knew, Her eyes are bright as dia - monds, they spar - kle like the
D7
G
C
dew. You may talk a - bout your dear - est maids and sing of Ros - y
G
D7
G
Lee, But the yel - low rose of Tex - as beats the belles of Ten - nes - see.

GIT ALONG LITTLE DOGIES

TRADITIONAL

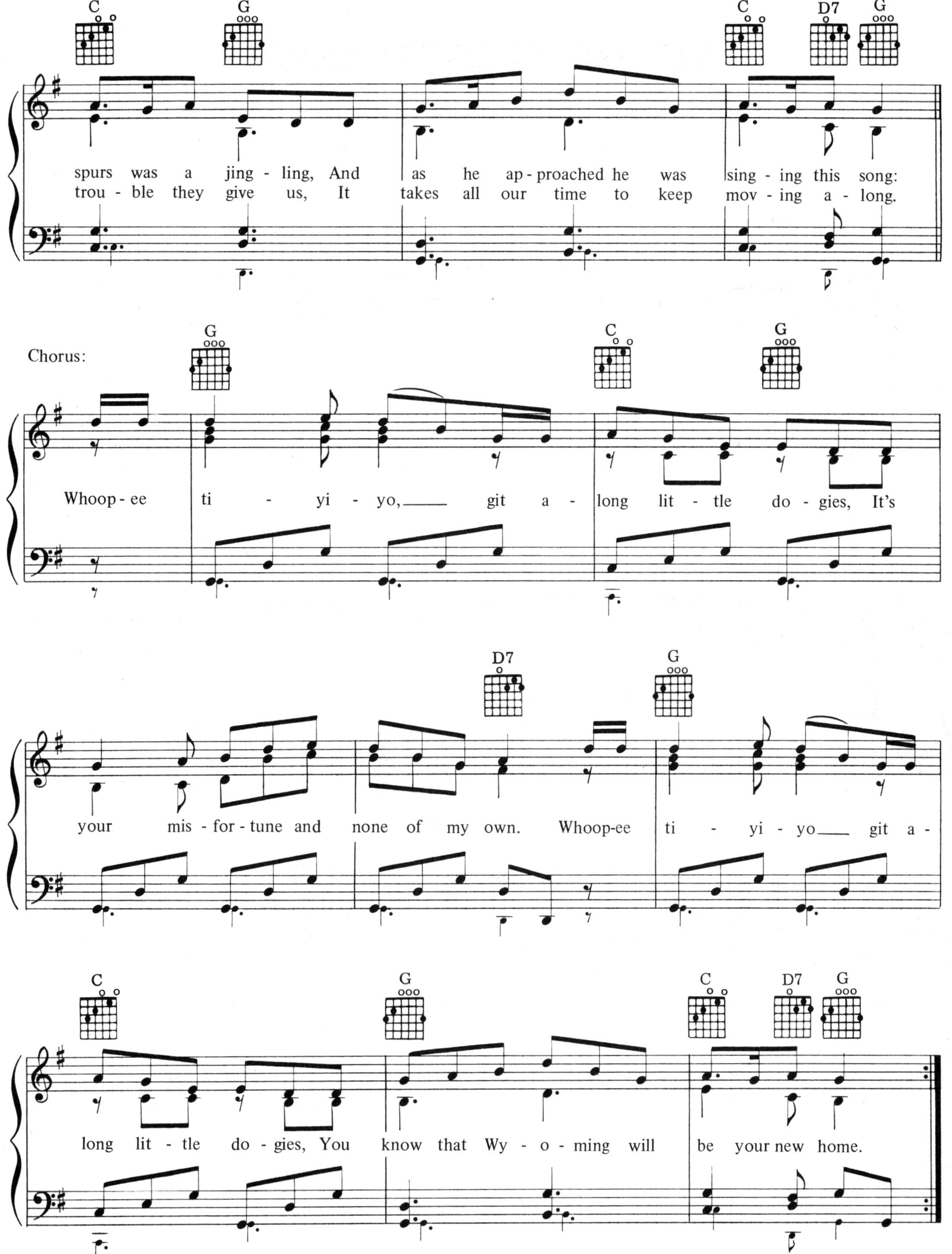
C
G
D7
spurs was a jing - ling, And as he ap - proached he was sing - ing this song:
trou - ble they give us, It takes all our time to keep mov - ing a - long.
Chorus:
Whoop - ee ti - yi - yo, git a - long lit - tle do - gies, It's
your mis - for - tune and none of my own. Whoop-ee ti - yi - yo git a -
long lit - tle do - gies, You know that Wy - o - ming will be your new home.

HOME ON THE RANGE

TRADITIONAL

G
D7
G
skies are not cloud - y all day.
G
D7
G
Em
Home, home on the range,
Where the deer and the
mf
A7
D
D7
G
an - te - lope play.
Where sel - dom is heard a dis -
C
G
D7
G
cour - ag - ing word And the skies are not cloud - y all day.
slower

SCARBOROUGH FAIR

TRADITIONAL

Additional Verses

3. Tell her to make me a cambric shirt
Sing parsley, sage, rosemary and thyme
Without any stitching or needlework
And she shall be a true love of mine.

4. Tell her to wash it in yonder dry well
Sing parsley, sage, rosemary and thyme
Where water ne'er sprung nor a drop of rain fell
And she shall be a true love of mine.

5. Tell her to dry it on yonder sharp thorn
Sing parsley, sage, rosemary and thyme
Which never bore blossom since Adam was born
And she shall be a true love of mine.

GREENSLEEVES

TRADITIONAL

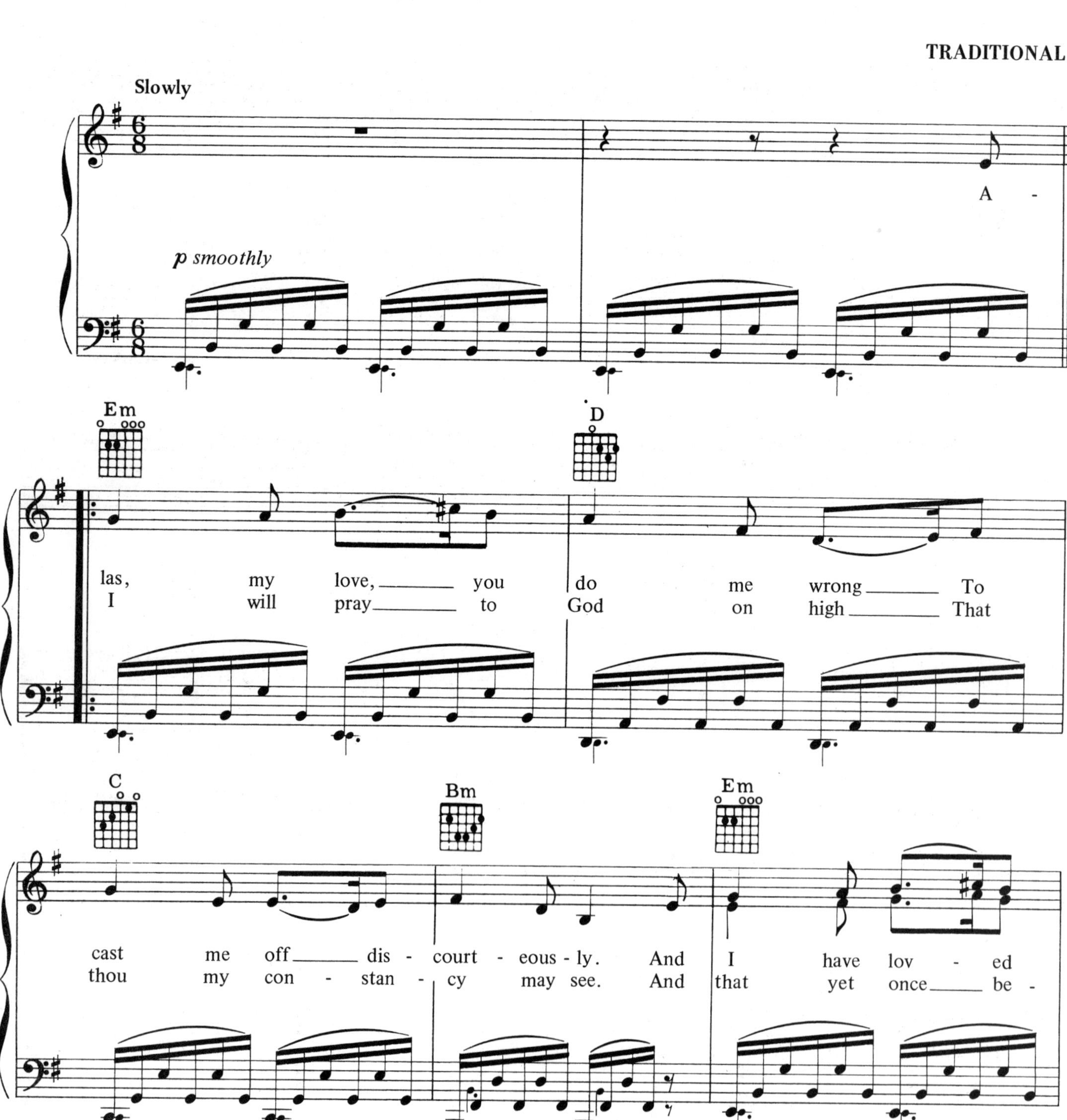

D
C
B7
Em
you so long, De - light - ing in your com - pa - ny.
fore I die, Thou will vouch - safe to love me.
G
D
Bm
C
Am
Green - sleeves was all my joy, Green - sleeves was
Bm
G
D
Bm
my de - light, Green - sleeves my heart of gold, And
C
B7
1.
Em
2.
Em
who but my La - dy Green - sleeves. Green - sleeves.

SHENANDOAH

TRADITIONAL

DOWN IN THE VALLEY

TRADITIONAL

Moderately slow

G D7

Down in the val - ley, val - ley so low,

G

Late in the eve - ning hear that train blow.

D7

Hear that train blow - ing, hear that train blow,

G

Hang your head o - ver, hear that train blow.

Roses love sunshine, vi'lets love dew
Angels in heaven know I love you.
Know I love you, dear, know I love you
Angels in heaven know I love you.

Write me a letter, send it by mail
Send it in care of Birmingham jail
Birmingham jail house, Birmingham jail
Send it in care of Birmingham jail.

WORRIED MAN BLUES

TRADITIONAL

G
sing a wor - ried song, It takes a wor - ried man
I lay down to sleep, I went a - cross the river
wrapped a - round my leg, Had twen - ty links of chain
to sing a wor - ried song I'm wor - ried
and I lay down to sleep And I woke
a - wrapped a - round my leg And on each
D
D7
C7
now, but I won't be wor - ried
up with shack - les on my
link an in - i - tial of my
1.2. G
D7
3. G
G7
long. I
feet.
name.

C. C. RIDER

TRADITIONAL

G
see what you have done: Now you
raised your win - dow high. But I
D7
C7
made me love you, now your man's done
shoulda kept walk - in', walk - in' right on
1. G
Tacet
D7
come. Now wom - an, you
2. G
Tacet
G9
10fr
by.

THE BOLL WEEVIL

TRADITIONAL

Tacet
Tex - as, just a - look - in' for a place to stay. Just a - look - in' for a
seen him he had all of his fam - 'ly there. Just a - look - in' for a
far - mer with a pair of blue duck - in's on. Just a - look - in' for a
D7
1.2.
G
home, just a - look - in' for a home.
home, just a - look - in' for a home.
home, just a - look - in' for a
Tacet
The
If
3. G
home. Just a - look - in' for a
D7
G
home, ain't got no home!

FRANKIE AND JOHNNY

TRADITIONAL

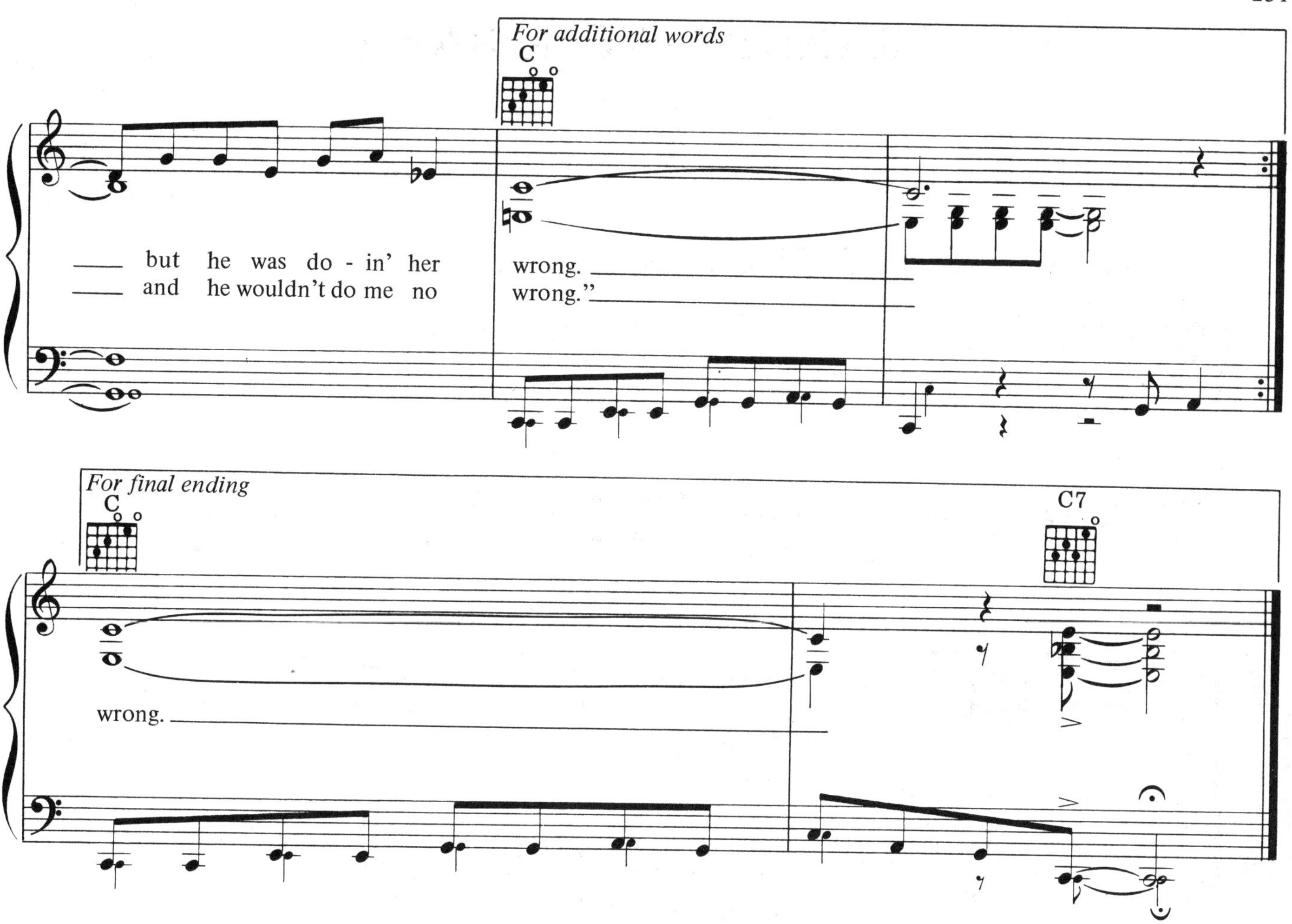

Additional Words

3. "Don't want to cause you no trouble,
Don't want to tell you no lie,
But I saw your lover 'bout an hour ago
With a girl named Nellie Bly.
He is your man, but he's doin' you wrong."

4. Frankie went down to the pawnshop,
Bought a small forty four,
She aimed it at the ceiling,
Shot a big hole through the floor!
"Where is my man, 'cause he's a-doin' me wrong."

5. Frankie looked over the transom
And found to her great surprise
That there on the bed sat Johnny
A-lovin' up to Nellie Bly.
He was her man, but he was doin' her wrong.

6. Frankie drew back her kimono,
Took out her small forty-four.
Root-a-toot-toot that gal did shoot
Right through that hardwood door.
She shot her man, 'cause he was doin' her wrong.

7. Frankie went down to his coffin,
Sadly looked down at his face,
Said, "Lord, have mercy on me,
I wish that I could take his place."
He was her man, but he was doin' her *(to final ending)*

MY OLD KENTUCKY HOME

STEPHEN FOSTER

1.
G/Dbass
D7
G
2.
G/Dbass
D7
birds make mu-sic all the day. The
old Ken-tuck-y home good-
G
C
G
G
C
G
D♯dim
night.
Weep no more my la-dy, Oh,
Em
C
G
weep no more to-day. We will sing one song for the
C
G
N. C.
G/Dbass
A7
D7
G
C
G
old Ken-tuck-y home, For my old Ken-tuck-y home far a-way.

JOSHUA FIT THE BATTLE OF JERICHO

A7
none like good old Josh - u - a at the bat - tle of Jer - i -
'round that cit - y sev - en times and the walls will tum - ble
Dm Aaug Dm
cho. That morn - in' Josh - ua fit the bat - tle of Jer - i - cho,
'way. That morn - in'
A7 Dm7 Dm
Jer - i - cho, Jer - i - cho, Josh - ua fit the bat - tle of
A7 Dm Aaug Dm
Jer - i - cho and the walls came a - tum - bl - in' down!

YOU'LL NEVER WALK ALONE

Words by
OSCAR HAMMERSTEIN II

Music by
RICHARD RODGERS

Moderately

mp very smoothly

C

When you walk through a storm hold your

sim. throughout

G/Bbass — F/Abass

head up high And don't be a-

C/Gbass — G — Gm

fraid of the dark. At the

Dm — Bb — F

end of the storm is a gold - en

Dm
B♭/Dbass
F/Cbass
Gm/B♭bass
F/Abass
sky And the sweet sil - ver song of a
E/G♯bass
C7/Gbass
F
lark. Walk on through the
Fdim
C/Ebass
Fm6
wind, Walk on through the rain, Tho' your
C/Gbass
Em
F
dreams be tossed and blown.

G7
C
Eaug
Walk on, walk on with
cresc.
F
D/F♯bass
C
Eaug
hope in your heart And you'll nev - er
Fmaj7
F♯7
Em/Gbass
G7
C/Ebass
Eaug
walk a - lone, You'll nev - er
ff
F
G7
C
Fm6
C
walk a - lone.
dying away
pp

BLUE BIRD OF HAPPINESS

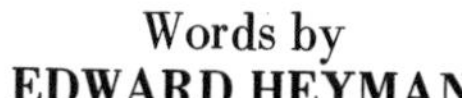

Words by
EDWARD HEYMAN

Music by
SANDOR HARMATI

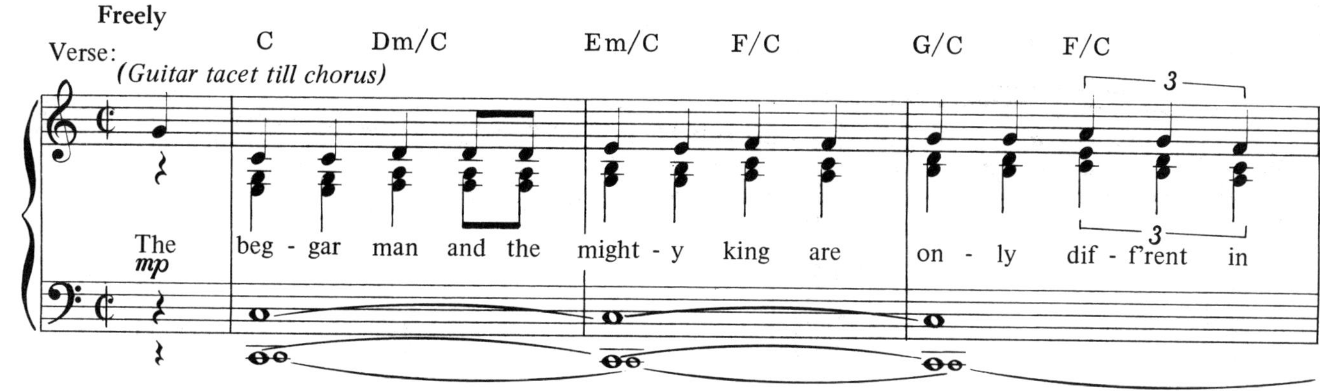

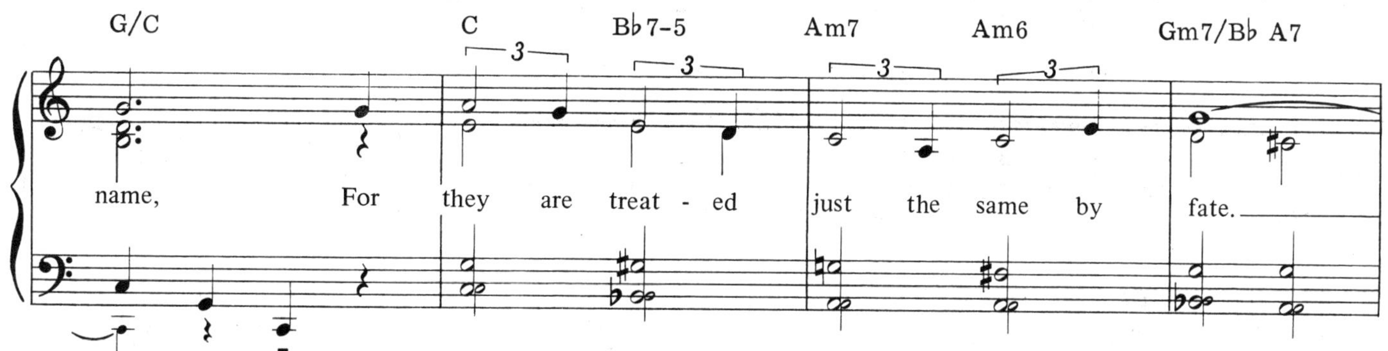

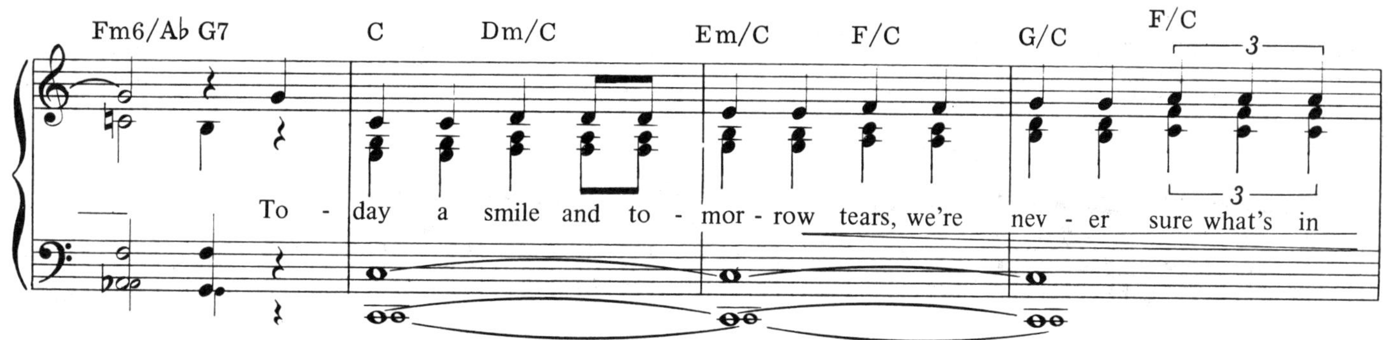

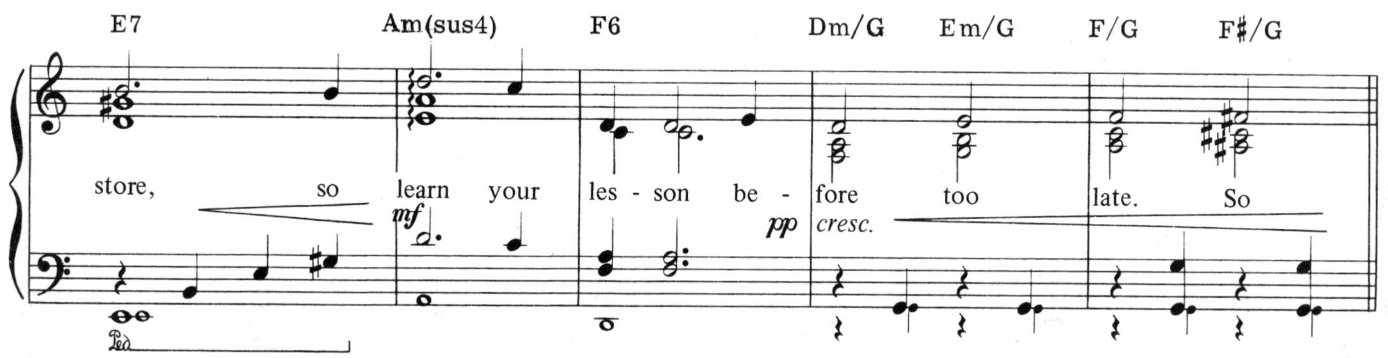

Moderately (without dragging)
Chorus:
Cmaj7
G11
Cmaj7
G11
be like I, hold your head up high
Life is sweet, ten - der and com - plete
mp
Cmaj7
Fmaj7
G11
C
Till you find a blue bird of hap - pi - ness.
Since we found the blue bird of hap - pi - ness.
Em
B7-9
Em
B7-9
You will find great - er peace of mind
When it's night ev - 'ry - thing seems bright
mf
Em7
Am7
D7
G
G7
Know - ing there's a blue bird of hap - pi - ness. And when he
Since we found the blue bird of hap - pi - ness. Two hearts that

C
E7
F
A7
sings to you Though you're deep in blue
beat as one 'Neath a new found sun
Dm7
G
G7
C/Ebass
E♭dim
G11
You will see a ray of light creep through. And so re -
We are in a world that's just be - gun! And when our
Cmaj7
G11
Cmaj7
G11
mem - ber this, life is no a - byss,
youth is gone, love will lin - ger on
Cmaj7
Fmaj7
G11
C
Some-where there's a blue bird of hap - pi - ness.
Since we found the blue bird of hap - pi - ness.
2nd time, slower

LOOK FOR THE SILVER LINING

Words by
BUDDY DeSYLVA

Music by
JEROME KERN

Cmaj9 C6 G11 G13-9 C6
heart full of joy and glad - ness Will al - ways
C11 C7-9 Fmaj7 F6 Fmaj7 E7-9 E♭+11 D9
ban - ish sad - ness and strife So al - ways look for
D13-9 Em7 Em7-5 Em7-5/Abass A7+5 Dm7-5
the sil - ver lin - ing And try to find the
Dm7-5/Gbass G7-9
(Guitar tacet)
sun - ny side of life.

AMAZING GRACE

TRADITIONAL

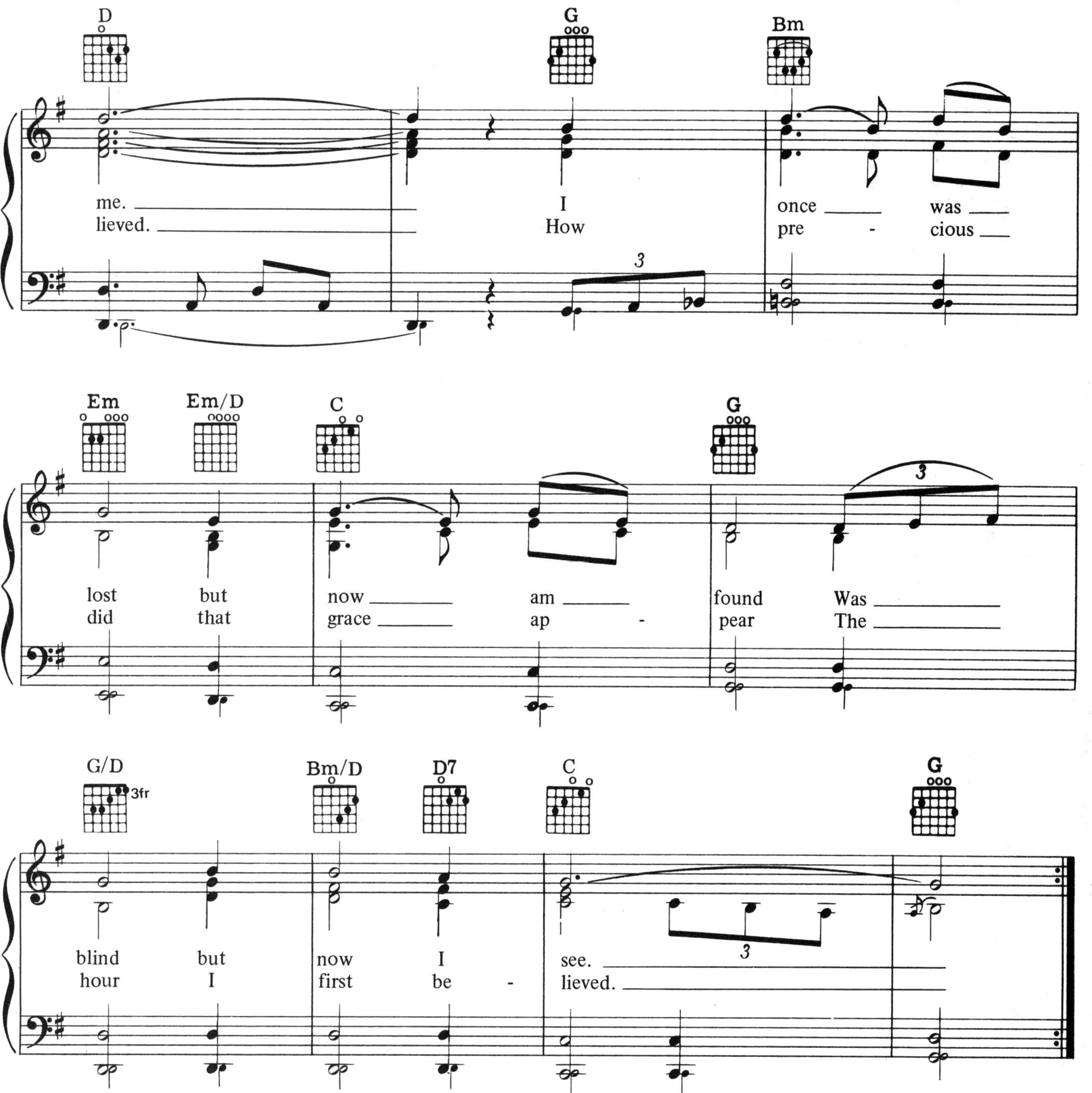

Through many dangers, toils and snares
I have already come
'Tis grace hath brought me safe thus far
And grace will lead me home.

Yea, when this flesh and heart shall fail
And mortal life shall cease
I shall possess within the veil
A life of joy and peace.

THE CHURCH IN THE WILDWOOD

3. From the church in the valley by the wildwood,
When day fades away into night,
I would fain from this spot of my childhood
Wing my way to the mansions of light.
(Chorus)

DOWN BY THE RIVERSIDE

C
G
stud - y war no more, I ain't gon - na stud - y war no more, I ain't gon - na
D7
G
G7
C
stud - y war no more. I ain't gon-na stud-y war no
G
D7
more, I ain't gon - na stud - y war no more, I ain't gon - na stud - y
1.
G
2.
G
war no more. 2. I'm gon-na more.

WHAT A FRIEND WE HAVE IN JESUS

Words by
JOS. SCRIVEN

Music by
C.C. CONVERSE

F/C
B♭/C
F/C
C
for - feit, O what need-less pain we bear,
faith - ful Who will all our sor-rows share?
sake thee? Take it to the Lord in prayer!
held back a little
F
B♭
Bdim
All be-cause we do not car - ry
Je - sus knows our ev - 'ry weak - ness;
In His arms He'll take and shield thee;
F/C
C
F
D.S. 𝄋
Ev - 'ry-thing to God in prayer!
Take it to the Lord in prayer!
Thou wilt find a sol - ace there.
After 3rd verse only
F/C
B♭
F
mf
softer and softer

HE'S GOT THE WHOLE WORLD IN HIS HANDS

TRADITIONAL

With a moderate swing (♫ to be played like ♩ ♪)

WERE YOU THERE?

YOU'RE A GRAND OLD FLAG

Words and Music by
GEORGE M. COHAN

G C G D7 G D7 G
heart beats true un - der Red, White and Blue Where there's
E7 Am N. C.
nev - er a boast or brag. But "Should
G5 D7 N. C.
Auld Ac - quaint - ance Be For - got," Keep your
A7 Am7 D7 G
eye on the grand old flag.

BATTLE HYMN OF THE REPUBLIC

Words by
JULIA WARD HOWE

TRADITIONAL

B7
Em
loosed the fate - ful light - ning of His ter - ri - ble swift sword. His
read His right - eous sen - tence by the dim and flar - ing lamps, His
Am
G/Dbass
D7
G
Chorus:
G
truth is march - ing on.
day is march - ing on.
Glo - ry, glo - ry Hal - le - lu - jah,
mf
C
G
Glo - ry, glo - ry Hal - le - lu - jah,
Glo - ry, glo - ry Hal - le -
B7
Em
Am
G/Dbass
D7
1.
G
2.
G
lu - jah! His truth is march - ing on. I have on.

AMERICA THE BEAUTIFUL

Words by
KATHERINE LEE BATES

Music by
SAMUEL A. WARD

Slow and stately

Additional Words

O beautiful for patriot dream that sees beyond the years
Thine alabaster cities gleam undimmed by human tears.
America, America, God shed His grace on thee
And crown thy good with brotherhood from sea to shining sea.

CLEMENTINE

TRADITIONAL

OH! SUSANNA

By STEPHEN FOSTER

G7
rained all night the day I left, the weath - er it was dry; The
if I do not find her, then I'm sure - ly bound to die, And a -
C C7 Fmaj7 Fm6 C G7 C
sun so hot I froze to death, Su - san - na don't you cry.
when I'm dead and bur - ied, oh, Su - san - na don't you cry.
F C G7
Oh, Su - san - na, oh don't you cry for me, 'Cause I've
mf
C C7 Fmaj7 Fm6 C G7 C
D.S. to 2nd verse
come from Al - a - bam - a with a ban - jo on my knee.
2nd time slower

CHICKERY CHICK

Lyric by
SYLVIA DEE

Music by
SIDNEY LIPPMAN

C
G7/D
C/E
G7/D
C
Be just like the chick - en who found some - thing new to sing:
D7
G7
C7
C+
O - pen up your mouth and start to, say, oh!
F
C7/F
Chick - er - y chick cha - la cha - la, check - a - la rome - y in a ba - nan - i - ka
F
F/E♭
B♭/D
B♭m/D♭
F/C
C7
F
bol - li - ka wol - li - ka can't you see chick - er - y chick is me

HUSH LITTLE BABY

TRADITIONAL

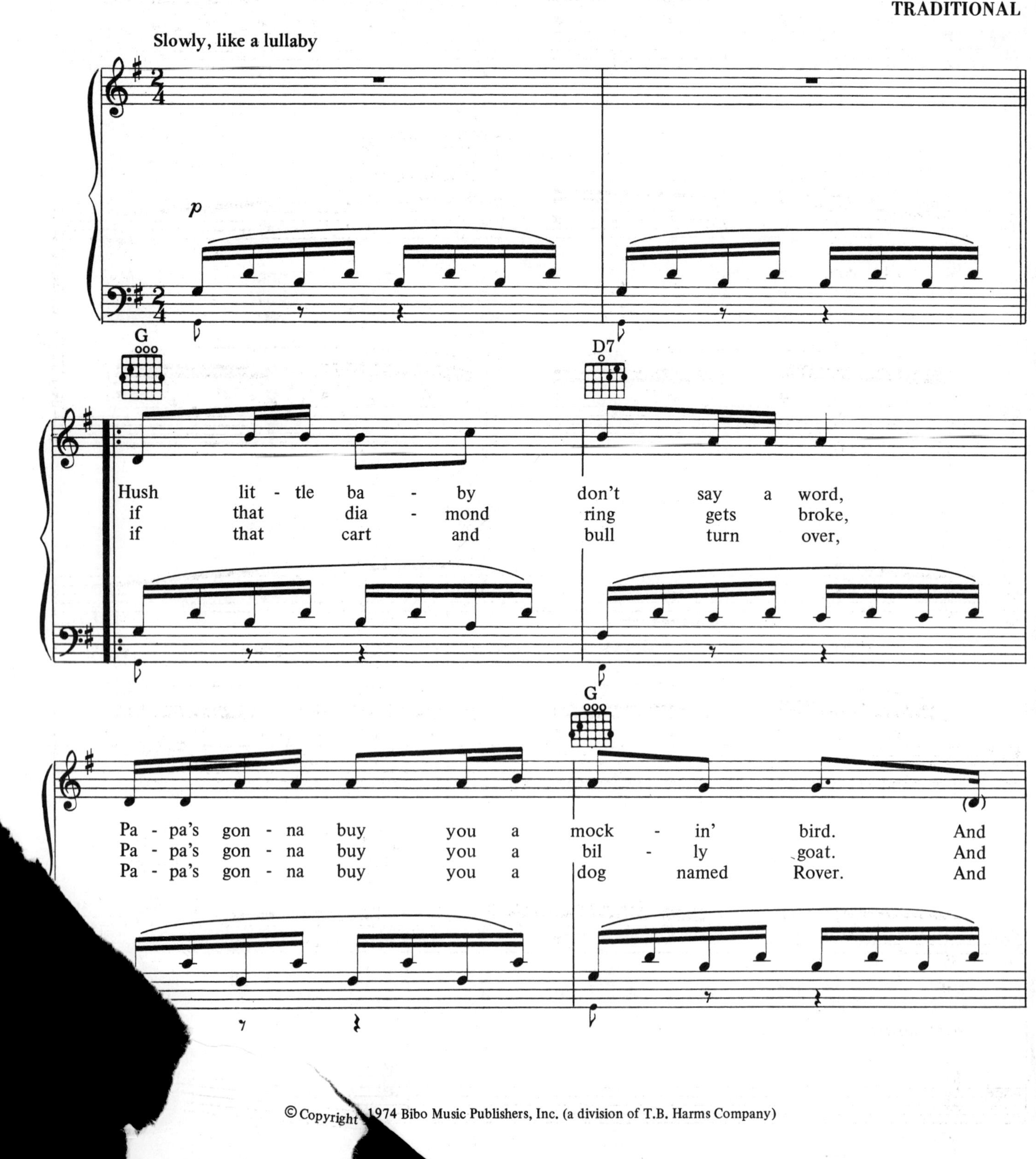

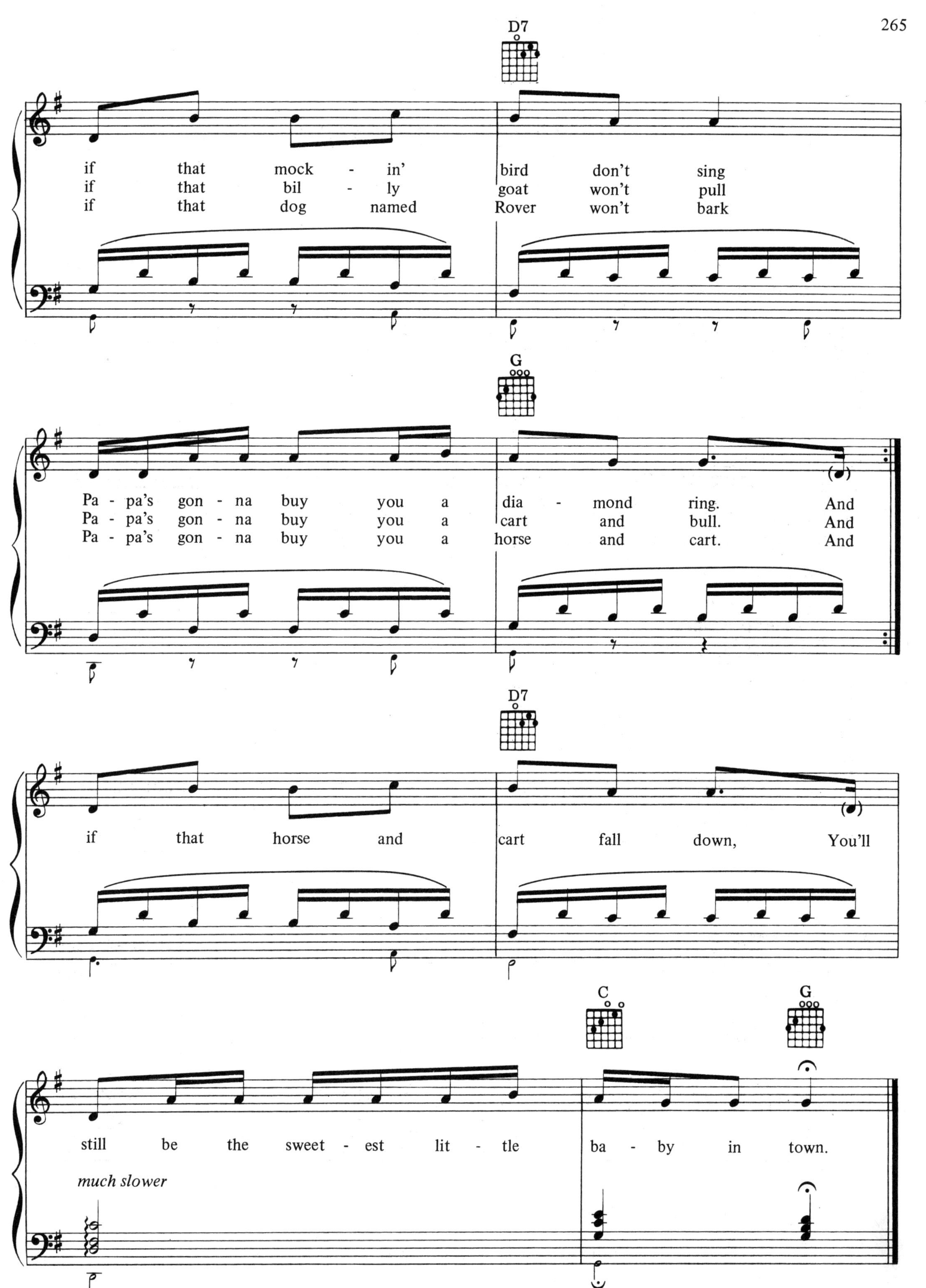
D7
if that mock - in' bird don't sing
if that bil - ly goat won't pull
if that dog named Rover won't bark
G
Pa - pa's gon - na buy you a dia - mond ring. And
Pa - pa's gon - na buy you a cart and bull. And
Pa - pa's gon - na buy you a horse and cart. And
D7
if that horse and cart fall down, You'll
C
G
still be the sweet - est lit - tle ba - by in town.
much slower

OH DEAR, WHAT CAN THE MATTER BE?

TRADITIONAL

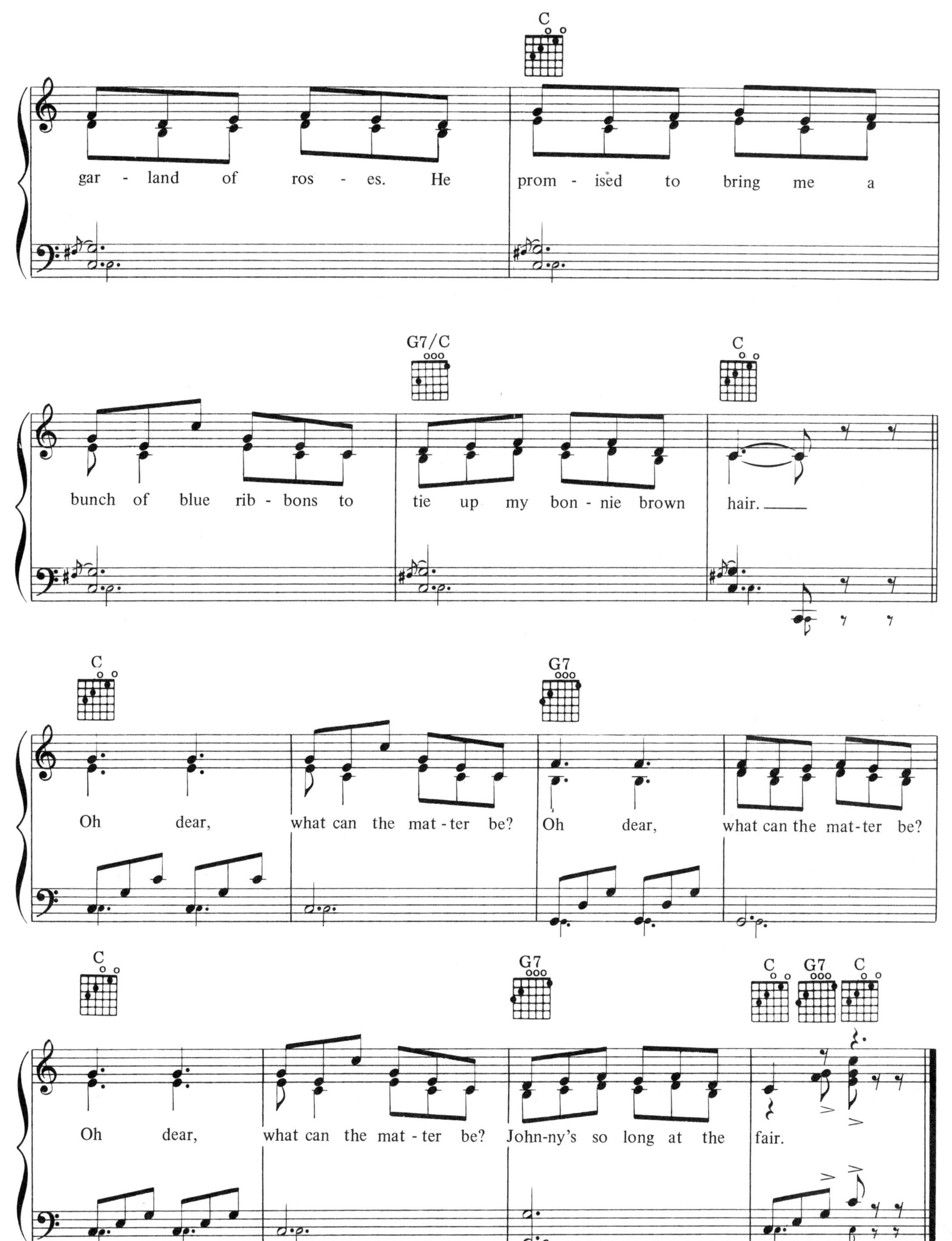
C
gar - land of ros - es. He prom - ised to bring me a
G7/C
C
bunch of blue rib - bons to tie up my bon - nie brown hair.
C
G7
Oh dear, what can the mat - ter be? Oh dear, what can the mat - ter be?
C
G7
C G7 C
Oh dear, what can the mat - ter be? John - ny's so long at the fair.

JINGLE BELLS

By JOHN PIERPONT

Chorus:

G

night. Oh! Jin - gle bells, jin - gle bells, jin - gle all the

C G A7

way, Oh, what fun it is to ride in a one - horse o - pen

D7 G

sleigh. Oh, jin - gle bells, jin - gle bells, jin - gle all the

C G D7 G

way, Oh, what fun it is to ride in a one - horse o - pen sleigh. Hey!

OLD MacDONALD HAD A FARM

TRADITIONAL

Continue with pigs (oink, oink), turkeys (gobble, gobble), etc.

LAWRENCE WELK THEME SONG

ADIOS, AU REVOIR, AUF WIEDERSEHN

Lyric by
JACK ELLIOTT

Music by
GEORGE CATES

G
B7
C
E7/B
Am
night, sleep tight, and pleas-ant dreams to you, Here's a
D7
D11
Gmaj7
G
wish and a prayer that ev-'ry dream comes true, And
Bm7-5
E7
Am
Cm6/E♭bass
now 'til we meet a-gain, A-di-
G/Dbass
D11
D7
G
os, au re-voir, auf wie-der-sehn.